# METAMORPHOSIS

*My path to transformation*

YVES CÔTÉ &
ALANA ABRAMSON

Suite 300 - 990 Fort St
Victoria, BC, V8V 3K2
Canada

www.friesenpress.com

**Copyright © 2021 by Yves Côté & Alana Abramson**
First Edition — 2021

All rights reserved.

No part of this publication may be reproduced in any form, or by any means, electronic or mechanical, including photocopying, recording, or any information browsing, storage, or retrieval system, without permission in writing from FriesenPress.

ISBN
978-1-03-910163-0 (Hardcover)
978-1-03-910162-3 (Paperback)
978-1-03-910164-7 (eBook)

1. *Biography & Autobiography, Criminals & Outlaws*

Distributed to the trade by The Ingram Book Company

# TABLE OF CONTENTS

# DEDICATION

To my dear brother Luc,
who passed away in 2020.
You are the reason for my awakening.
I love you with all my heart.
RIP my dear Brother.

# GRATITUDE

Self-publishing of *Metamorphosis* was made possible by the generous support of the following donors and other anonymous contributors. Thank you for making a dream become a reality.

Ian & Elaine Abramson, Tamara Abramson, Janet Adamson, Daniel Ackland, Noelle Anderson, Maggie Aronoff, Catherine Bargen, Jennie Barron, Christine Berger, Shannon Boyko, Lyle Brydges, Rachel Bunt, Ann Marie Carlson, Kim Cote, Alice Chambers, Chris O'Connor, Catherine Douglas, Mark Frederick, Ryan Friesen, Nikita Hiebert, Randy Hind, Rev Donald Ibsen, Jessica James, Sharon MacDonald, Patrick Rafferty, Arianna Marquez, Janna Materi, Charlotte Ribalkin, Kevin Merz, Larry Moore, Brenda Morrison, Gene Murphy, Karen Parhar, Leon Remus, James Reilly, Patrick Richmond, Nicole Ripley, Katie Rogers, Sharleen Rutledge, Natalie Sampat, Alyssa Shore, Zofia Switkowski, Bobbi Terrell, Mara Veneman, Richard Wainwright, and Krystal Wereta.

Sincere thanks to Grant Hartley who created the cover art #granthartleycreations.

# PREFACE: METAMORPHOSIS

One evening I was attending a group in a prison's chapel. A couple of volunteers told me they had five caterpillars in their fridge and that they were waiting for spring so they could film their metamorphosis. They explained that the caterpillar builds a cocoon and eventually transforms into a butterfly, breaking free of the confines of the cocoon and taking flight.

The whole time I was listening to this story of change, I could not stop thinking about the process that we must go through to become beautiful human beings ourselves. My personal transformation from being a violent, uncaring man to a loving, respectful person, is the journey I want to share. How does someone go from an innocent five-year-old child to spending almost 32 years in prison after committing countless acts of violence? How does that same person then return to the community as a responsible, contributing citizen?

This book is not all about recounting the heinous details of criminal violence, what has happened to me, what I have done to others. Rather, this book is about change. The title, *Metamorphosis: My Path to Transformation*, reflects this focus.

How many times in our life do we reach a fork in the road? I have faced many crossroads, and, over the years, these provided me opportunities for growth and change. I needed to make these changes to achieve new goals that I set for myself. Each fork in the road invites us to make decisions. Sometimes we may change our point of view, change our way of thinking, and even our image.

Chapter 1 provides an overview of my life. The chapters that follow contain some of my experiences and perspective on various topics including making change, friendship, love, religion, crime and punishment, incarceration, and reintegration. My life has been nearly 60 years in the making and I have a lot to say. For this book, I have selected the most impactful life experiences that I am able to remember. Like any memoir, this story is incomplete. My memories of many things have faded, and I have done my very best to represent significant life events in the way I recall them. This story is my truth and I do not speak for anyone else but me.

# CHAPTER 1 - WHO AM I?

## *Family History*

My name is Yves Réal Côté. I was born on November 12, 1961, in the county of Abitibi in the small village of La Sarre in the province of Quebec. I am of European decent and was raised by Catholic parents like almost everyone else in the village during that era. My biological mother's name was Marie-Claire Simard and she was also born in the Abitibi area. My maternal grandparents lived their entire lives on a farm in Val-Paradis which was known throughout Quebec or *La Belle Province* (the beautiful province) for its beautiful covered bridges. I would often admire a bright red bridge that stood out amongst the greenery that wound its way along the shores of the river.

My biological father's name was Antonelie Côté and he was from the small village of Petite-Rivière-Saint-François in the county of Charlevoix, Quebec. His family were native to this village and the hotel and restaurant my father built with his own hands became part of the town's infrastructure.

I am the second youngest of eight children—five brothers and two sisters. Unfortunately, although common at the time, another child died at birth. From the eldest to the youngest my siblings are Beavis, Wilma, Chester, Gille,

Dick and Jane (the twins), me, and Luc.[1] I don't know any of my siblings very well for reasons that will soon become clear. My biological family were essentially strangers to me with the exception of Luc. We had always stayed in touch and spent close to 10 years together in prison.

Beavis was the tallest of the family, had a slim build, and smelled terrible. His face was drawn and nearly skeletal, skin stretched taut over bone. He looked like a real creep, someone you couldn't trust. My disgust for his physical appearance as well as his actions made shooting him later in life seem like a reasonable choice. Beavis was the kind of guy that never failed to take advantage of a situation, often showing up to people's homes for a "visit" with all his luggage and no plans to leave until he was literally thrown out.

Wilma was the mother-figure and took responsibility for our youngest sibling, Luc. A tiny woman at 4 ft 11 in and three-quarters, she never let you forget about those three quarters of an inch that would make her nearly 5 ft tall. Wilma and her children escaped a violent husband and father. She divorced and I heard she went back to school and became a laboratory technician.

Chester wanted to be known as a womanizer. He saw himself as a playboy, but he didn't really have the charm to back it up. Although we share some similar features, he was a chubby narcissist who didn't look after himself.

Gille was the intellectual amongst us and, unlike Chester's delusional "good looks," Gille could back up his smarts. Athletically built and trustworthy, he was the only one of us who attended university. He obtained a business degree from the University of Ottawa, married, and had children. He and Wilma were the only ones out of the eight of us who lived a non-criminal lifestyle. Recently, I learned that Gille passed away in 2012 while I was in prison. I never had ill-will toward Gille and I felt hurt, disturbed, and angry that nobody in my family tried to contact me when he died.

I didn't meet the fraternal twins, Dick and Jane, until I was a teenager. Jane was, in a word, evil. She would belittle our youngest brother, Luc, destroying his self-esteem with her taunting words. Luc would often break down in tears and, eventually, she broke him. I blame both her and me for the criminal lifestyle he later ended up in. Dick was a drama king, overreacting

---

1 In order to protect privacy, some names have been changed.

to everything. I didn't like the twins; one was a pure bully and the other was a spineless worm.

My parents are both dead. My mother, Marie-Claire, died in 1967 when she was only 34 years old. She was a teacher who dreamt of being a doctor. My father had been putting money aside for her to study medicine. I was only five years old when she died and have only a few vague memories of her. I remember her looking like a "typical mother" with a round face, medium build, and glasses. Until my mother's passing, I think I had a pretty normal childhood. She was nurturing to her children and I can remember holding hands with her as we watched my father build a house.

My father, Antonelie, was a reserved man. He always wore a white shirt and tie even when he worked on cars or fixing things around the house. My father was almost a complete stranger to me. I don't remember us ever sitting down and having a conversation. Our encounters were brief and felt almost professional as he played the role of a father the way many men did in those days: cold, direct. My father was an authority figure whom I feared. One day I wanted to go out and he said, "If you leave, I will punch you in the head." I said something rude and went to walk out the door. He got up from his chair and punched me in the head. This punch was hard, calculated, controlled, and unemotional. This was my father's way.

My father's demeanour did not waiver when he told me my mother was dead. I had been playing in my grandparent's barn with some of my siblings. I ran towards my father when I saw him. He crouched down, placed his hand on my shoulder and told me that "mommy was dead and gone to heaven." I still remember the feeling like being hit by a truck. Sadness came over me and I started to cry. He did not console me. He remained stoic in the months that followed, including standing graveside where my mother was to be buried. She died in winter but wasn't buried until spring as the ground was too frozen to dig up.

My parent's relationship appeared to be loving and close. Her sudden death devastated all of us. My father was left alone with five children under the age of eight while trying to run his business. My father mourned the loss of my mother and would remind me to make the sign of the cross in her memory whenever I passed a cemetery. Later in life, I remember doing this subtly while being in a car with a social worker. I dipped my head down and looked out the window as my fingers crossed my forehead and chest. The worker noticed and said if I was embarrassed, I could make the sign more discreetly with my thumb to my palm. I remembered this lesson and continued to make a tiny cross whenever I passed a cemetery when others were around.

Soon after my mother died, I was sent to live with relatives for about a year. Unable to raise eight children alone, my father arranged foster care for most of my siblings through the Children's Aid Society in the Ottawa region. The eldest boy, Beavis, Wilma, and Luc, the youngest, stayed at home with my father. Wilma helped take care of Luc, who was only 18 months old. The twins remained together in the same foster home as my brother, Gille. For the most part, I was separated from my siblings and spent the biggest part of my childhood in foster care in the Ottawa, Ontario region and my adolescence in Charlevoix County, Quebec. I spent a little time in foster care with my older brother, Chester, and my youngest brother, Luc. But much of my upbringing, I was raised by strangers.

Like most of us, there are events from my childhood that affect me to this day. Losing my mother and being separated from my siblings were things I didn't choose, and I felt terribly alone. My mother's traumatic death in my childhood paved the way from being an innocent, happy child to a cold, violent criminal.

One of my first memories is of abandonment. I was standing on the sidewalk one sunny day on St. Patrick Street in Ottawa. It was late afternoon and I must have been 5 or 6 years old. I am watching the traffic pass in front of me and, in a flash, I see a black sedan suddenly stop across the street. My father sticks his head out of the drivers' window and yells, "Yves!" while waving at me. He drives off as fast as he had appeared. This image is burned into my mind along with the feelings of happiness, sadness, and confusion all at once. It happened so fast that it seems like a dream.

## Life in Foster Care

At 6 years old, I was placed in my first foster home with my older brother Chester who was about ten years older. My youngest brother, Luc, also stayed there for a while. I lived in that foster home until I was nine or ten years old.

Although my memories prior to the age of 6 are fuzzy, I remember everything about being in the hell of this foster home. I will never forget what the family looked like, the colour of the house, address, yard, and details of the inside. I live with the scars of how I was treated there to this day.

*House of hell*

I believe I would have been better treated had I been the family pet rather than a child of 6. When I asked for water or anything to drink, the lady refused these requests; she felt I had to go to the bathroom too often. It's true I often went into the bathroom, but it wasn't to urinate. I went to the bathroom to drink from the toilet. I was so scared of the abuse that would come if they learned I was drinking from the sink that I would drop to my knees in front of the toilet and scoop water with my hand to my lips. Toilet water has a very distinct taste.

The family had three children of their own: one teenage girl, a little girl who was about the same age that I was, and a son who was a few years younger than I. Their own kids were treated much differently than I was; they were allowed to move freely around the house and to take what they wanted from the fridge.

I was hit with a yard stick in the basement for disobedience, but the mental abuse always felt worse than the physical beatings. I would be sent to bed early and then hear the doorbell ring. The cheers, laughter, and smell of pizza that followed confirmed I was a household nuisance rather than a human being.

During my time in this house, I was often on the kitchen floor or in the yard. It was from that kitchen floor that I saw what normal family life looked like. One of the foster "parents" favourite punishments was to order me to face the corner on my knees. I spent hours on those cold tiles, my knees turning red and then purple. To this day, I have issues with my knees and cannot have any direct pressure on them. From the kitchen floor I learned that there was no need to cry. My tears meant nothing to that family. I would ask myself, "What is wrong with me? Why am I not a part of this family? What is going on here?" I was confused watching the other children being treated differently than I was. I was shown no signs of affection like hugs, kisses, or sitting on laps while watching TV.

Other small and rather strange things stand out from my time in foster care. For example, every day I would have a tomato sandwich sent with me to school. That sandwich was usually made the night before and when I opened it at lunch time, the bread was soaking wet and mushy. I told the lady at the foster home many times that I didn't like tomato sandwiches. However, she would keep on making them as if to spite me. To this day, I hate anything to do with whole tomatoes. I love ketchup and spaghetti sauce, but the sight of a tomato makes me ill.

Chester was able to come and go as be pleased and never protected me. For the short time that Luc was in that foster home, he was treated with the same cruelty. At this young age, I noticed that adults were hypocrites. I remember when the social worker came to visit the house the lady running the foster home was actually nice to me! I could sit at the table and a glass of juice or milk and cookies would appear in front of me out of nowhere. Once social services left, I was right back on the kitchen floor. I began to lose a sense of self-worth, self-esteem, and trust in others. I felt defective, unloved, and worthless. I lost a lot of myself in that foster home.

What disturbs me to this day about this part of my past is how so many red flags were ignored. How is it possible that I was left alone to deal with this kind of abusive behaviour from the people who were given the responsibility for my well-being? The first time I got kicked out of school I was in Grade 2. I had trashed the principal's office in a temper tantrum. RED FLAG. I ran away from the foster home several times before the age of nine. RED FLAG. I stood on a pile of snow, yelling that I did not want to go back to school or the foster home. RED FLAG. I was transferred to multiple schools because of excessive behavioural problems. RED FLAG. These red flags and countless others were ignored by everyone around me: social services, teachers, principals, physicians, neighbours, and my own older brother, Chester.

Around the age of nine or ten I was moved to another foster home and none of my siblings were there. This lady was an older widow whose husband had died. She had a couple of children of her own. This lady was nice; however, by the time I was sent to live with her, I was already "damaged goods." I had been in at least five different schools and kicked out for fighting. I ran away from this home several times and would fight other kids right in front of the house. Even at that young age my behavior was becoming bloody.

Due to my increasingly violent behavior, social services placed me in a group home for teenagers when I was 11. This was another turning point in my life as I was the only French speaking kid out of the six residents in the home. I couldn't speak English and none of the staff spoke French. I learned very quickly how to speak English to communicate with staff so I could eat. I am thankful that my little brain was like a sponge and learning a new language seemed easy. I became completely bilingual, which made me defiant in both languages. It was around this time I started getting involved in crime with some of the older kids in the group home. Although I was influenced by some of the kids around me, my behaviour was always the most extreme.

# *Youth Detention*

At first, I feared the thought of being locked up. I was a very small child and wore glasses. The first time I stepped into a juvenile custody centre on Bronson Street in Ottawa, I was deathly afraid as I was led through the metal door into a concrete box. However, once I was locked inside that cell, the constant fear I had experienced since the age of five disappeared, and I felt safe. Being locked away in that cell alone meant nobody could abuse me. Although I was threatened by some of the other youth, I was used to fighting people my age. The adults in the jail never abused me and my physical needs for shelter, food, and medical care were met. As for my emotional needs, I had given up on those years ago. Institutions became safe havens for me, and I no longer feared getting arrested, charged, and sentenced.

From 11 to 13 years old, I would alternate between spending time in the group home and juvenile jails for shoplifting, running away, bicycle theft, car theft, vandalism, and skipping school. I stole my first car and was charged with a firearms offence at 13 when I pointed a rifle at the police. No matter how many times I was arrested, I just kept doing crime and returning to jail. On the rare occasions I saw my siblings or my father, they rejected me. Despite my young age, my violence made them fear me.

At 13 years old, I was displaying such destructive behaviour I was placed into the psychiatric ward of the Royal Ottawa Hospital. I spent about nine months there under the care of a psychiatrist. I didn't understand why I was in the hospital as I didn't feel sick but being there reinforced my belief that I was abnormal, stupid, and defective.

Youth in the psychiatric wing of the hospital were securely housed in round, two-story buildings. The main floor was an open area with the staff offices, kitchen, dining area, and bathrooms along the perimeter. Upstairs were the pie-shaped bedrooms and an open carpeted space in the center where group therapy and other activities took place. I had a captain's bed with drawers underneath, which I thought was so cool. I went to school on the grounds of the hospital and was treated kindly by a teacher. I was given medication every day in the form of little blue pills. I was told the medication was to keep me calmer. I had violent tantrums where I would be held down by staff.

A few times during my stay, I had wires attached to my scalp that were hooked up to a machine. Sometimes the wires were taped onto my scalp, and other times some sort of pin jabbed painfully into my skin. I was asked questions during these sessions as the doctor watched the machine. I never did know what they were doing or why, but strangely this wasn't the first time I had probes in my head. I remember having the same procedure at a younger age, and this gave me the impression that there was something very wrong with me.

Nothing that happened in the hospital helped me, although I felt safe there. When the time came to be released, I was offered two options: be put up for adoption or to move back in with my father. I chose to go back to my father to avoid anything that looked like the abuse of my past foster homes. For me this was a new adventure, a new beginning.

At 14, I moved back to Quebec into the house of a stranger from my past and a new stranger. My father had remarried a woman who had no children of her own. I knew nothing about her except that she had an identical twin and worked as a cook at my father's restaurant. I respected her because she was my father's wife, but there were many awkward encounters. Shortly after I moved in, she gave me a bath. She treated me like I was a child, bathing me as if I couldn't do it myself. I felt humiliated, ashamed, and confused. The experience reinforced my belief that I must be abnormal or retarded.

The only siblings staying at my father's house were Gille and Luc. A short time after arriving, my father and I went from Quebec City to Ottawa to attend family court so he could regain custody of me from the Children's Aid Society. In the long hours of this road trip and after all that had happened, we should have had a lot to say to each other. This was not the case and we remained silent for most of the trip.

At one point, we stopped for a meal at a café inside a gas station off the highway. My father got some sleep in the front seat of his black Oldsmobile Delta 88 Royale. I sat, wide awake, in the back seat. I wasn't able to sleep because I was afraid my father might molest me. Although my father had never abused me, I was so accustomed to authority figures mistreating me I expected it from him too. Looking back, I realize that my dad wasn't a predator, but as a child who was sexually abused so many times, that's where my mind went. I had learned nobody could be trusted.

I stayed with my father and stepmother from the age of 14 and a half to 17 and a half. I was never able to adapt to this new environment and I never fit in. I didn't stop doing crime or using violence. I spent two 6-month sentences in juvenile jails around Quebec City and 10 months in another jail across the river from Quebec City in Lauzon, Quebec. I also spent some months in a psychiatric ward, temporary foster homes, and living on the streets. In the 3-year period I was supposed to be "living at my father's," I spent very little time there.

For a short time, I lived in Jonquière, Quebec, with my brother, Beavis, and his wife, where they fought constantly. I was smoking cigarettes, which my brother stole from me and forbade me to smoke. I would work at a neighbour's farm shovelling manure in the early hours before school. Beavis would take all my earnings, verbally abused me, and, often, hit me really hard just to see how far I would fly.

The last foster home I was in was when I was 16. Shockingly, the Ministry in Quebec placed me in a house on the outskirts of the village with a single male in his late 20s or early 30s. The house was located less than 30 kilometres from my father's home. I thought this foster parent was cool because he was young and let me drink and smoke pot with him. He would bring me to bars when I was obviously under age. He would get me drunk and high, and when I fell asleep, I woke up to him raping me. This happened on numerous occasions. I felt ashamed, dirty, betrayed, and neglected. Just when I thought I met someone who cared, life proved otherwise. To make things worse, I came to learn that he was sexually abusing some of the neighbourhood boys too. He used to let the boys ride his snowmobile, and these kids didn't know the high price they would have to pay. Eventually, this man came to fear me as I became more and more aggressive. I ran away and took constant feelings of rage and frustration with me.

Between the ages of 5 and 17, I was in many different foster homes, juvenile custody centres, and a couple of psychiatric hospitals. I really didn't mind being locked up in institutions as they were the only place I was able to adapt, rest, and feel a sense of belonging. The world outside meant abuse and violence. Institutions gave me what I was missing and needing: a sense of safety and belonging. I now understand this to be "institutionalization."

At the age of 17, I began working on the ships. These bulk carriers were located on the Great Lakes and the Saint Laurent River. I navigated for three years, until the end of 1981. In 1983, after my first release from prison, I returned to work on a ship for 3 months in the sea of Beaufort in the Arctic Circle. I loved it as it was an adventure and a completely new experience for me. Working on the ships gave me the structure that I needed at that time in my life. I had also chosen a life where I would not have to bother with good-byes, which had been so painful in my past. I knew that for a sailor it was important to be able to change ports without caring about leaving anyone behind. I isolated myself for protection, which was something I learned from the abuse of the past.

I have no childhood friends. Not by choice, but because I moved so often. For most of my life, the person I was closest to was Luc. I had respect and unconditional love for him. Respect is such a simple thing, but at times it is so difficult to receive and give. For me, respect means treating people as you wish to be treated and don't do to others what you wouldn't want done to you. This is often easier said than done. When we were children, this respect motivated me to defend Luc as I was never protected. We lived through a lot of suffering together because of the abuse we both experienced during our time in foster care. We only had each other for comfort after being harshly punished but always managed to get through things together.

Sadly, Luc and I were not always together during our youth. Too often, circumstances separated us. Our deep connection did not happen overnight but developed through both painful and joyful times. We laughed, cried, and faced our fears together. We shared everything and when we felt threatened, we killed together.

Just like me, Luc was an innocent child when our mother died. He had the potential for a very different life. He had a unique sense of humour and cared about me when nobody else did. Even in the hostile world of prison, he managed to make me laugh to the point of having stomach cramps. I am happy to say that, unlike me, he is not doing a life sentence and became a free man.

I have no memories of my grandparents, aunts, uncles, or cousins, I have always been distant from family and relatives. I never really had a connection with my siblings. I have absolutely no tolerance or patience for any other member of my family except for my eldest sister, Wilma. I admire her for the way she has brought up her two children and lived her life. After I shot my older brother Beavis, our relationship ended. I lived in so many foster homes, juvenile centres, psychiatric hospitals, and prisons that all family connections have been terminated.

I believe that one of the reasons that human beings have been able to survive throughout history is our ability to adapt to almost any situation. I adapted to the foster homes I was in. Because of my history in juvenile correctional settings, I also adapted very well to life in adult prisons.

## *Entering the Adult System*

I had just turned 20 in November of 1981 when I decided to take the money that I had made working on the ships and travel to Jamaica for a holiday. The vacation ended when I was imprisoned for two weeks for marijuana possession. It was one of the only times in my life I can say I was not guilty of the charges I faced. Prison in Jamaica was nothing like I had experienced in Canada. I was the 13th man in a cell no larger than two regular cells and we had only a five-gallon bucket to relieve ourselves in. I was ferociously beaten for the first four days and the police raided my hotel room and took my money and most of my belongings while I was imprisoned. To ensure my release, I pled guilty and paid a fine. I could not get out of that country fast enough, boarding a plane to Ottawa the day of my release with two black eyes and a bad attitude.

Fueled by a sense of injustice and the feeling I had nothing to lose, I wanted to settle the score with my eldest brother while I was in Ontario. Growing up, Beavis was abusive to me, my siblings, and our father. He was a bully and extremely cruel. I wanted him dead and convinced three of my brothers to help. When Beavis met us at our father's house, we kept him hostage for three days. During that time, we all beat him repeatedly. I watched over him, torturing him by hitting him and threatening to kill him. On the third day, I grabbed his head, tilted it back, put his own gun under his chin, and shot him.

Beavis didn't die that day. He survived and testified against all four of us. One brother and I received a 42-month sentence for attempted murder, forcible confinement, extortion, and the use of a firearm during the commission of a crime. My younger brother, Luc, was sent to a juvenile centre and another brother received two years in prison.

From that adult sentence in January 1982 until December 2013, I was only out of prison for about 11 months. The first time I was released was in 1983; I was out for 5 months, in 1986 for 3 months, and for 3 months in 1989. I was 27 years old during that last release on mandatory supervision, which is what happens once you have served two-thirds of your sentence. The idea of early release is to ensure there is community support and accountability on parole and in a halfway house, rather than just hitting the streets straight from the toxic world of prison.

In 1989, I was released directly from Millhaven Institution, which is a maximum-security facility in Ontario. I was unable to cope with the cultural shock of going from this institution to the community. Millhaven, like most maximum-security facilities, was extremely structured. Prisoners are told when to wake up, when to take medication, when to work, when to shower, and when to sleep. We were told what, when, and where to eat. Leisure activities (exercise yard, common room time, and canteen) were also structured. The lights stayed on all night in some institutions, which made it difficult to sleep. Everything was clockwork, and every day was the same. If we needed to see the doctor or our parole officer, we filed a paper request and sometimes waited for weeks or months.

In addition to structure, maximum-security means violence is omnipresent, and the culture was clear: trust no one. We lived in defensive mode, were constantly on alert, and any signs of weakness were preyed upon. This is a culture I was familiar with living in abusive homes and being placed in institutions. With each incarceration, I became less able to function within the community and more comfortable in prison.

I had difficulty finding employment due to my criminal record and lack of education and employable skills. It was nearly impossible for me to meet people and form meaningful relationships because of my lack of social skills and history of abuse. Outside of prison, I wandered aimlessly, feeling lost and alone. I was depressed and used alcohol and drugs to overcome my introversion, suspicion, and shyness. I was never successful moving from prison to the community where there was no structure, unpredictable days, and you needed to trust people. Within 3 months of my last release, I was back inside pre-trial jail facing a first-degree murder charge.

It seems unthinkable for most people to imagine taking a life; however, the violence I used that ended a man's life was planned and deliberate. At the time, I wanted to return to prison forever and I knew that committing murder would achieve that goal. I didn't care about anyone, including myself, and I knew that being a murderer would be the perfect defense mechanism. I was done with being a victim of abuse. People who commit murder are feared by everyone—both inside and outside prison—so all I needed was a suitable victim. In my mind, the person I chose to kill was someone nobody would miss. He had neither a wife nor children, was an ex-convict, owed me money, and didn't deliver on his promise to help me when I got out of prison.

A week before the murder, I met up for coffee with an old acquaintance from prison. He was involved in the drug trade, and while we got caught up, he told me he had a pump-action shotgun. I was intrigued, and told him I had a 22 semi-automatic pistol and planned to use it to kill. I suggested that the two of us and the victim go to a deserted road off the highway outside of Ottawa to fire those guns. He could stay in the car while I followed through with the murder. He agreed.

On the morning of the murder, it was cloudy. I called my co-accused and he picked me up. We loaded the weapons into his car. I called the victim and invited him to come with us to try the firearms out. We picked the victim up in my friend's red New Yorker sedan and drove to the site. My victim and I got out of the car and I told the driver to stay in the car for now. The victim and I went for a walk down the road. We walked side by side on opposite sides of the street. I turned toward my victim, lifted my sawed-off shotgun, pointed it at him, and shot twice. The first bullet hit his lower side and when he turned the second shot entered the left side of his chest. He fell to the ground. I took out the semi-automatic 22 pistol and shot him four times in the head, point blank. I went back to the car, put the weapons in the trunk, sat on the passenger's side, and said, "Let's get the fuck outta here. It's done."

A few hours later, we drove to Mississauga, Ontario, west of Toronto. While in Mississauga, we robbed the same bank twice, exactly one week apart. We used the exact same weapon I had used to take a man's life.

In both robberies, I entered the building with a shotgun, shot into the ceiling, and told everyone to "get the fuck down!" My co-accused went teller to teller collecting money while I guarded the door. I cannot imagine the horror of the bank tellers who were unlucky enough to be on shift during both robberies. One of the bank clerks testified in court that when she saw us coming in one week after the first robbery, she said to herself, "Oh no, not again!" Someone managed to escape the situation. When I was manning the door and my co-accused was collecting the money, I heard the door open behind me. I turned around and saw a young Asian woman walk in. She looked at me and I shook my head "no." She immediately turned around and walked out. When my co-accused and I left the bank in a hurry, he went right and I went left. As I was walking away, I saw the woman who had almost been a victim of the robbery and said, "Bad timing, that's all," and kept walking.

I didn't intend to hurt any innocent people. I really had no idea the trauma I was causing as, in my mind, I was only hurting myself. I had a clear plan to be caught, which was apparent to both me and the authorities. I did nothing to cover my tracks: I didn't conceal the body, left shell casings behind, kept the murder weapon, and used it to commit other crimes. I was setting myself up for the only life I knew I could handle: a life in prison.

After the robberies, we returned to Ottawa to pick up some things. Only a few hours after arriving in the city, we were sighted by the Ottawa police, and a car chase was underway. We ditched the car, and a foot pursuit continued; I went one way, and my co-accused went the other. A police officer shot at me and missed, but I tripped and was immediately arrested.

On September 22, 1989, I was arrested and charged with first-degree murder. Fourteen months later, I was given a life sentence without the possibility of parole for 25 years. The sentence of "life 25" replaced the death penalty, which was abolished in 1976. This is the most severe sentence in Canada and is handed down when the killings are found to be planned and deliberate. Two days after receiving this sentence, I got another 14 years for two bank robberies and an additional year for prison breach for attempting to escape from the Ottawa-Carleton Detention Centre while awaiting trial for my first-degree murder charge. On December 20 or 21, 1995, I received another life sentence without parole eligibility for 15 years. This sentence was for second-degree murder after I killed another prisoner in 1993 in Donnacona Institution near Quebec City.

I have come to understand that all the violence I have used in my life has been instrumental, calculated, goal-oriented. The first murder gave me a life sentence and the second murder gave me status, which meant protection inside prison. The victim was a loud mouth to staff and other prisoners and would scream obscenities on the range. Like many in prison, he took advantage of others. It was all part of the game. He would borrow video games from weaker prisoners and sell them. When the meals came onto the range, he would keep his leftovers, wash them off, and sell them to unsuspecting, hungry prisoners. He was not well liked, nor respected. However, you don't need a good reason to kill in prison. Violence is so tightly woven into the culture, it is expected. When I decided I would send a message to everyone by killing this man, I did not hesitate. As soon as the bars opened, I sent Luc into his cell and followed behind him. We both assaulted him, and then as Luc kept watch, I used a putty knife turned into a shank and a 10-inch nail to carry out this despicable, selfish deed. To keep people away from me, I demonstrated to the prison population that I would do anything.

Afterwards, I left his cell and walked down the long corridor towards the gym. I passed by two guard stations on my way. They never noticed the blood on my running shoes or splatters on my face. Once I got to the gym, a friend told me to wash off my face and glasses.

This gruesome killing set the stage for my life sentence. In the theatre of prison, I was afraid but couldn't show it. I was looking at 25 years inside, so I needed to send a clear message that I was not to be messed with. In the grim reality of prison culture, this worked, and I was not victimized in the three decades I was locked up.

# CHAPTER 2 - JUSTICE

In 2015, the Minister of Justice and Attorney General of Canada, the Honourable Jody Wilson-Raybould, conducted a Criminal Justice System Review, which included a series of roundtables with justice system partners and interested parties from across Canada. One of the most consistent themes that emerged from this review was that those who come in contact with the criminal justice system are vulnerable or marginalized individuals. They are struggling with mental health and addiction issues, poverty, homelessness, and prior victimization. Most felt the criminal justice system is not equipped to address the issues that cause criminal behaviour in these groups, nor should it be. Participants felt these issues are worsened by an over-reliance on incarceration.

These critiques of the system are not new and certainly relate to Yves' story. Many people like Yves are ignored as victims only to be later punished as offenders. In turn, the majority of the millions of dollars related to Yves' movement through the system have been spent on the astronomical security costs related to incarceration, not on support for his victims nor his rehabilitation. Canadians pay high economic and emotional costs for "justice," yet most who encounter the system are neither satisfied nor report an experience of justice. Elliott (2011) has noted that Canada has a "legal" system, not a "justice" system.

The question of what justice is has stymied moral philosophers, legal scholars, and citizens for centuries. Despite dubious claims that punishment is effective in changing behaviour (Elliott, 2011) when a rule or law has been broken, the assumption that punishment is the "right" thing to do remains the status quo. While the public and media often use the term "justice" as synonymous with "punishment," justice is not something that can only be measured by years of incarceration.

Justice says something about societal values and how we should treat one another. Justice is about promoting the overall health and well-being of people and acknowledging that "we live in relationships with others but also that relationship and connection with others is essential to the existence of the self" (Llewellyn & Downie, 2011, p. 4). Justice cannot be reduced to how the system responds solely to the harm-doer when a law is broken. Rather, justice can be understood as a response to harm that seeks to address the needs of all.[2]

How do I see the justice? What do I think of justice system? I thought I would know a lot more about justice after serving 32 years, but I really don't have many answers. While Canada has one of the best legal systems in the world, it is not without serious defects.

The criminal justice "system" is composed of three distinct parts that do not work very well together: police, courts, and corrections. My contacts with police began early in life. When I was growing up, the police were just another authority figure; one that you had to run from if you had done something wrong. My experiences have been varied, and I have come across both ethical and crooked cops. As a youth, most police looked at me with pity as a lost child. I wasn't difficult to deal with and always kept my mouth shut. I knew they couldn't help me so I just accepted however they treated me. Unlike many ex-cons, I don't have hatred for all people who wear a uniform. I don't like to be stereotyped, so why should I stereotype others?

2 Author's note: Alana Abramson's introductions and conclusions are indicated by the following typographic break

Some of the more unfortunate experiences involved police officers putting forward false evidence in the hopes of convicting me. For example, during trial for the two bank robberies I committed in Ontario, I noticed that the amount of money the police claimed that was taken from the banks was much lower than the actual amount we took. Furthermore, they put forward a witness statement that contained conflicting information. At one time, the witness stated he saw me in dark sunglasses and then later claimed the look in my eye told him "I was going to kill everyone". The fact that these false claims could be used to convict me is troubling as it means those in law enforcement are not always honest.

After being apprehended by the police and charged, the next stage of the criminal justice process is attending court. Going to court is a cold, confusing experience. Being brought from my cell to the courthouse, I entered a universe that felt like I had lost all control over my fate. In this big room filled with strangers, the only people allowed to speak are the lawyers and the judge. The only time the accused is expected to speak is to plead guilty or not guilty. The accused is not required to take the stand to give their testimony if they don't want to. It is a rare occasion that the defence suggests that the accused give evidence to avoid a conviction. Once the verdict has been determined, the convicted person can say a few words prior to being sentenced by the judge. In my experience, most accused stay silent throughout the entire court process.

Many people believe that most crime is committed by the lower class. They are quick to judge the character of the silent figures in the prisoner's box. However, offences are committed by all classes of society. I have done time amongst millionaires and people who have lived on the streets. But those with money, or people locked up for corporate or white-collar crimes are few. Most people locked up are from the most marginalized groups in society. I have analyzed these injustices and seen evidence of how conscious and unconscious bias affects the decisions of so many people in the system: lawyers, judges, jurors, and witnesses.

The Crown Prosecutor is the lawyer who puts forward evidence on behalf of the Government of Canada. The prosecutors' performance is evaluated by the number of convictions they achieve. Being on the receiving end of many Crown lawyers' convictions, I find it hard to see their humanity. I felt they lacked honesty in many of their arguments, but I also know they are just part of a bigger system with lots of problems.

To protect the rights of the accused in the adversarial court process, those criminally charged have the right to a defence counsel. For those who cannot afford to hire a lawyer, the government appoints legal aid counsel. That means the accused must place their future into the hands of someone they have never met and who is paid much less than private lawyers. Criminals like me are suspicious by nature and it is difficult to trust that appointed lawyers have our best interests at heart. Mostly, I felt I was just another "file" for them to deal with as quickly as possible.

Serious and violent offences, such as those I was charged with, can take a very long time to move through the labyrinth of the legal system. The delays are very stressful for everyone and, unfortunately, the services provided by legal aid in Canada are pitiful compared to those offered through private law firms. The idea that "you get what you pay for" is true across many services.

For a good notary, you must pay the price. Reliable and honest mechanics are only accessible with good money. However, there is a critical difference between requiring the services of a mechanic and a defence lawyer. With the latter, your freedom is at stake. The quality (or lack of quality) of a criminal defence impacts the accused, the victims, and society at large. Although the social class of an accused person does not make him more or less dangerous, many wealthy people have avoided incarceration for vicious crimes because they were able to hire an expensive lawyer.

I sometimes had the privilege of being represented by lawyers who were people of honour. A good lawyer will not sell you out to reach a deal with the Crown but will give you informed advice. Even though I was found guilty in most of my court cases, my lawyer was not bad. I was guilty.

Guilt or innocence is determined by either a judge or a "jury of my peers." Juries are composed of 12 people who I am sure would never speak to me in the street. These citizens understand little or nothing about the law, but my fate is in their hands. I always found this scary when I considered the errors experts like judges have made with respect to wrongful convictions. I don't have bitterness for jurors because I know they are obliged to serve.

Judges play the role of arbiter in the justice theatre. They read reports about me, interpret facts about things I am accused of doing, and apply the law. Since my first time in front of a judge at 11 years old, my perception of the court has been the same. I felt humiliated, deprived, and powerless as I watched strangers argue about my future.

Usually I was silent in court as my lawyer always told me to keep my mouth shut. However, one time before being sentenced for bank robberies, I was not able to hold my tongue. I felt silenced by the legal process so many times and wanted the chance to express myself to the authorities. I turned and faced the public gallery and said, "The sentence I am going to receive here today is not important to me because, just 2 days ago, I received a life sentence. I will not be eligible for parole until I serve a minimum of 25 years in a penitentiary. I think that it is long overdue for society to revaluate their priorities when rapists walk free and those who steal your money are put behind bars."

I was expressing my disgust towards a system that was not able to keep me safe as a child and continued to fail victims. Naturally, the judge expressed disapproval of what I said and gave me 14 years for the bank robberies and one for trying to escape prison.

Since 1982, I have been in 18 different federal institutions: two super-maximum institutions (known as Special Handling Units or the SHU), five maximum institutions (Archambault, Donnaconna, Edmonton, Millhaven, Renous), seven medium institutions (Drummondville, Federal Training Centre, Macaza, Joyceville, LeClerc, Mission, Stony Mountain), two minimum institutions (Ferndale, St. Anne), one Regional Treatment Centre (RTC), and a multi-level Regional Reception Centre (RRC). In Canada, people sentenced to anything over 2 years serve their time in federally run facilities. The federal government ministry responsible for corrections is called the Correctional Service of Canada (CSC). Each province operates institutions that house people serving less than 2 years or are on remand, awaiting their day in court.

There are significant differences between federal institutions and those run by provincial governments. I was never sentenced to anything less than 2 years; therefore, the only time I have spent in a provincial institution were short stints on remand while awaiting trial. The longest period I spent in a provincial institution was 14 months. What I will write about incarceration is based on my experience in federal institutions.

Many people wonder why I have been in so many different institutions. The reasons are complicated—sometimes the placements were voluntary, but most often they were based on policy and prison politics. Canada is divided into five regions: Pacific, Prairie, Ontario, Quebec, and Atlantic. Each region has its own institutions. Often where the crime took place determines where you will do your time; because I was sentenced in both Ontario and Québec, I did time in these provinces. However, I also have been the subject of involuntary transfers outside of these regions for involvement in jailhouse politics, which means I have done time in the Prairie and Atlantic regions. I voluntarily transferred to British Colombia in 2003 to finish my sentence close to Luc and eventually make a new life for myself in the community.

I have experienced a great deal in the 32 years I was locked up. I have seen riots, homicides, suicides, escapes, assaults, and overdoses. Unfortunately, I have been a participant in some of these. Over the years I became numb to violence as I have seen horrors that human beings should never witness.

When I first entered adult prison, I was scared to see the gun towers and hear guns being shot for unknown reasons. When I heard the steel door shut behind me, I was terrified. The bang of my cell door closing rattled my bones. I never liked loud noises and still don't. However, our human capabilities for adaptation are incredible. After a while, it got to a point where I couldn't wait for that cell door to close. My cell became my comfort zone. After many years of incarceration, you get to love your solitude. I find it strange that a human—meant to be social and free—can adapt to being locked up in a room that is the size of a walk-in closet.

To deal with my fear of an adult federal prison, I looked around the prison yard and asked myself what I was afraid of. What scares me the most in here? Being in a maximum-security prison, there were a lot of big, mean looking guys. As a young 20-year-old who was only 5 ft 7 in and 130 lb, the guys working out all the time both scared and impressed me.

The guys with tattoos all over their arms and bodies scared me too. Prior to the 1990s, only certain groups had tattoos: sailors, soldiers, bikers, and criminals.

The guys serving time for murder were also scary, especially those in serving life sentences for first-degree murder. Those murders were considered "planned and deliberate," so they were not an accident. There were men who used violence to get their message across or to get other people to do what they wanted, men that murdered other prisoners.

Fast-forward 10–15 years: I am in prison serving two life sentences, one for first-degree murder and one for second-degree murder. I'm 5 ft 7 in and 225 lb, and my body is covered with tattoos. I have been working out for 20 years and was known as one of the strongest men in most of the institutions I have served time in. I have used violence while in prison as an instrument to get what I want. I became like the men that I feared when I first entered prison.

At the beginning of my life sentence, I thought that if I did my time quietly and not get involved in anything, my stay would be short, and I would not have any problems. It was a mistake to believe that doing time would be that simple. Being in prison reinforced the values of the criminal world and made me view the outside in distorted ways. I learned to listen to and study this prison world, and as I did so, the world outside slipped away.

Doing time quietly was perceived negatively by the institutional authorities. They claimed they could not get to know me. When I decided to get involved in prison life more actively, I chose to participate in institutional politics, such as being part of the inmate committee and the underground economy. Then the authorities accused me of being too visible and a disruptive influence within the prison population, and I was transferred. This felt unjust, as did most of my experiences in the system. These feelings of injustice often distracted me, taking up the spaces in my mind where I should have been considering the impact of my actions on my victims.

I will never debate or complain about the sentences that I received over the years. I was a very violent man who needed to be stopped. I am accountable for the crimes I committed and do not blame others for my actions. I have made some very bad choices in my life and am paying a high price for these decisions. However, prison does not automatically equal justice and we need to stop pretending it does. Very few people who commit a crime are ever caught and, if they are, those with financial resources will often beat the charge. This means most of us lose with the current legal system.

During my incarceration I would often remember that nobody has ever taken responsibility for the abuse I experienced as a child leading directly to my violent behaviour. In considering this topic of justice, I am left with more questions and no answers. What is justice, then, and who is it for?

Whose needs should be addressed? Are victims experiencing justice? Does justice look the same for everyone? Where is the justice for all the victims of childhood abuse and neglect? Who is accountable? If not individuals, what about the social systems that continue to fail the most vulnerable in society?

Perhaps justice is not an event but a process. I am seeking to bring about justice to my many victims by committing to a life without violence. To that end, I have lived outside of prison for nearly 7 years. I got married and secured employment. I am involved with some activities that are part of my Christian beliefs. I volunteer and help others inside and outside of prison. I am living the best life I can with the demons that haunt me. The following chapters cover topics that have been important on my journey including the experiences of imprisonment, serving a life sentence, transformation, fear of release, and reintegration.

It is easy to locate many examples of where the justice system has failed child victims like Yves only to punish them later as offenders. As unjust as these cases are, it is difficult to imagine how the legal system alone can address the complex biological, psychological, social, economic, structural factors, and inequities that relate to harm and violence. The 2015 federal government's criminal justice system review found that Canadians recommended:

- The legal system must be made *fair*, *efficient*, and *compassionate*, using evidence and sound information.
- There was a need for different approaches for people with *mental illness and addictions*, as well as the overly high numbers of vulnerable and marginalized people in the criminal justice system.
- *Collaborative approaches* that partner with social systems, the private sector, and others in the criminal justice system are needed.
- There should be increased opportunities for and the use of *restorative justice.*
- *Victims' issues* should be addressed with compassion and fairness, allowing survivors of crime to be heard.

These recommendations can pave a path for conceptualizing justice very differently. Evidence about the use of incarceration, especially long-term sentences like the one Yves is serving, has long demonstrated this approach ineffective, expensive, and harmful. Justice that provides opportunities to transform people, relationships, and structures is much more promising. What if justice was about getting well rather than getting even? (Pranis, Stuart, & Wedge, 2003).

# CHAPTER 3 - LIFE FROM THE INSIDE

There is so much to be said about prison life. Time has opened my eyes and shifted my perception of corrections, the people who work there, and the policies that guide correctional practice. When I was first incarcerated, I felt that everyone deserved to be there, including me. I thought the way many Canadians still do: "Don't do the crime if you can't do the time." Over the years, I met people in prison who were there because of unmanageable and serious mental health issues and trauma. Through work on myself and talking with others, I started to come to terms with my own trauma and how it had affected my life. Perhaps our "choice" to use violence was limited due to the impact of trauma on the body and brain. There are many people that should not be punished in prison but need to be helped. The old, the sick, the vulnerable—it broke my heart to see the suffering all around me, with no end in sight. The help they needed should have been offered long before some prison program, taken because of coercion from your parole officer, and in which you are "programmed" under constant threat of violence by other inmates.

When it came to the staff when I first entered prison, it was "us" and "them." As I cascaded to lower levels of security and was able to have more open conversations with staff, I realized that they were human beings.

During the Violence Prevention Program, a 6-month high-intensity program for violent offenders, the psychologist and the program facilitator shared some stories of their own personal struggles. This allowed me to connect and have empathy for "them." I also met people working in corrections that had empathy for me. They wanted me to do well, to get out, and to succeed! I now feel that most people working in prisons are doing the best they can while working in a toxic, oppressive environment that breeds suspicion and prevents the development of healthy human relationships.

It is hard to understand the complexity of corrections through its technical, complicated language and countless acronyms. To add to the confusion, there are also historical, political, and contemporary aspects and constantly changing laws and policies. Corrections is made up of many actors including judges, lawyers, correctional officers, administrative staff, civilian workers, nurses, program facilitators, institutional parole officers, volunteers, psychiatrists, chaplains, elders, and researchers. There is also the lived experience of people like me who are experts of a different kind.

Readers might expect this chapter to be filled with details of the violent acts within prison: murders, suicides, riots, assaults. However, many books and TV shows of this nature already exist. Instead, I am hoping to present prison life in a way that those with the pleasure and privilege to live free can perceive this complex world. In this chapter, I hope to help readers understand the system by delving deeper into my personal experiences throughout a lengthy term of incarceration.

Upon receiving my sentence, I entered the federal system through the Regional Reception Centre (RRC). At RRC, I met with a classification officer who had me complete numerous psychological, academic, and attitude tests. Along with the results of these risk assessments, factors such as sentence length, the nature of the offence, treatment needs, and the number of previous incarcerations impact a prisoner's security classification. Whether an inmate begins their sentence in a maximum-, medium-, or minimum-level institution is determined by their case management team (CMT). The CMT includes the classification officer, a correctional officer, and a correctional supervisor. This team follows a prisoner for the duration of their institutional stay and recommends any changes in security level. This same team prepares correctional plans for each prisoner and, when the time comes, makes recommendations about parole.

Many people believe judges make decisions about which prisons inmates serve time in; however, judges only determine the length of sentence, not how or where it is served. The level of security is determined by the CMT and each level of security has unique qualities. Lower levels of security means inmates have more autonomy and access to rehabilitative programs. Higher security means more time locked up, no or fewer programs, and much more violence.

Security level classifications have serious implications to the person under sentence. One of the main causes of violence in prisons stems from people being classified inappropriately. For example, I have seen young men placed in a maximum-security prison to teach them a lesson or create fear. In maximum-security, there is a good chance this young person will be seriously messed with. Maximum-security institutions perpetuate hatred, and the threat of violence is ever-present. There is always a group of prisoners who are ready to do anything to prove what they are capable of. I know because I was once one of them.

When young people arrive in the unknown world of maximum-security, there are dangerous people who already have their routines established. Some younger guys play their music loud, shout and behave like children, and cry about their sentence. Often, they do not respect the routines of the other prisoners. Routine is very important in prison and some of the newer additions have to learn this the hard way.

It often seems that many young prisoners enter the system with the idea they can do whatever they want, but this is pure fantasy. There are rules and regulations to follow, even when there is no supervision from prison authorities. The most important rule is to respect your neighbour. There are two ways to learn this lesson about respect. The first is to simply realize that as we are living in a situation where it is essential to have some degree of harmony, one must respect the neighbours whom he did not choose.

The second way is to learn through extreme physical force. If somebody comes into an institution without respect, he will be made to understand. We don't call the prison authorities to settle misunderstandings, and even the biggest prisoner will be sent a pack of wolves to teach him respect. People new to prison quickly learn that people—especially those serving long sentences—only wish to do their time in peace.

Some people come into prison addicted to alcohol or drugs, often having committed crimes due to substance abuse. These prisoners can become increasingly afraid as they sober up and start to face the harsh reality of their situation. Sometimes, they feel the need to prove themselves, but they are not in a world where people turn the other cheek. On the street, it might be advisable to give way to the aggressor and not react. In the maximum-security world, it is the opposite. In the face of an aggressor, we fight to save face, or we risk being abused for the rest of our time inside.

Different levels of security produce striking differences in mentalities of both staff and prisoners. In a maximum, most prisoners are serving long sentences for things like murder, bank robbery, kidnapping, extortion, and high-level drug dealing. These prisoners are often dedicated to doing their time without any problems, so they can eventually go down security levels.

In institutions where the security level is not as high, there are a greater number of people serving shorter sentences or in on their first prison term. These "short timers" are often involved in violence as they seek to make a name for themselves. The nature of one's offence also matters more in high levels of security. In maximums and most mediums, sexual predators are kept away from the general population; otherwise, they will be the victims of very violent actions.

## The Routine

Here is the schedule of a typical day in a federal prison in Canada. Depending on the level of security, the amount of time spent inside your cell varies. The higher level of security, the more time you are locked in your cell. For example, in the highest level of security of the Special Handling Unit (SHU), prisoners will spend about 20 hours (and up to 23.5 hours a day) in their cell.

07:30 Opening of cell doors for breakfast; option to go to the common room or return to the cell to eat.

08:00 Opening of cell doors; exit cell for work.

11:30 Return to cell for an official count, which ensures all prisoners are accounted for.
12:00 Opening of cell doors for lunch; option to eat in common room or cell.
12:30 End of lunch and return to cell.
13:00 Opening of cell doors; exit cell for work.
16:00 End of work; return to cell for another official count.
16:30 Opening of cell doors for supper; option to eat in common room or cell.
18:00 Opening of cell doors for activities such as gym, gathering in the common room.
19:00 Change of activities.
20:00 Return to cell for another official count.
20:30 Opening of cell doors; exit for activities.
21:30 Change of activities.
22:30 Return to the ranges, end of activities; option to go to common room or cell.
23:00 End of all daily activities, return to cell. Final official count.

This routine is the same every single day. In prison, there are no holidays or birthdays. There might be small changes to the schedule on weekends or special national holidays, when limited activities replace work. Almost every day feels the same and boredom is a common enemy.

Most prisons across Canada have many cells that sleep two people. This practice is called "double-bunking" and is a cost-saving measure. Try to imagine sitting in concrete room measuring 6.5' to 7' for most of the day with someone else. As bad as it is to be alone, it can be worse to have company you didn't choose. Given my history of abuse, being placed in a locked cage with another man felt like an inhuman measure. I have had many, many cellmates over the years; I had to undress in front of them, smell their shit when they used the shared toilet, and listen to them sleep. I was never alone, and even a lover will tell you that they need time and some space. Our punishment is being deprived of our liberty; we should not be subjected to further punitive measures while doing time.

It is inconceivable and unacceptable to place two individuals in a cell designed for one. I filed a grievance in 1994 when double-bunking became mainstream. I claimed two men to a cell was against our *Canadian Charter of Rights and Freedoms* to be protected against cruel and unusual punishment. I maintained that double-bunking increased the risk of violence and eliminated privacy. As a result of this grievance, I met with the Commissioner of the Canadian Penitentiary Service at the time, Mr. John Edwards, and expressed these concerns in person. Mr. Edwards listened to these points and said they were valid and would be taken under consideration. More experienced prison staff were also opposed to double-bunking as they could see how it increased tension and, therefore, the risk of violence for everyone. However, the practice continues to this day. Even individuals like Mr. Edwards, who mean well and see our cause, are usually ineffective in making a change in this primitive, punitive system.

## *Correctional Staff*

Correctional officers or guards are often referred to by prisoners as "screws." They are hired to maintain the security of the institution and to support rehabilitation; our experience inside is greatly affected by how the staff treat us. I once saw people working in corrections as government employees who had reasonable ethics, like any other law-abiding citizen. However, doing time showed me a different angle as I observed many correctional staff abuse their power. For many years, it was difficult for me to trust a civil servant working in prison. Although this is changing, for years, it seemed that their main goal was to punish prisoners. Whether by pure meanness or ignorance, the damage done by staff to prisoners can be immense.

For example, one of the most humiliating things for anyone—men or women—is to be forced to strip completely naked in front of strangers. I understand the need for these kinds of measures in a so-called "secure" environment; however, strip searching should be limited. I have had experiences where I had been in segregation for a very long time with zero human contact or yard time when, out of nowhere, four to five correctional officers would appear two to three times a week to tear apart my cell, strip search me, and leave. It even happened when the only things in my cell were the bedding and the clothes on my back. It is impossible to overstate how traumatic this is to someone like myself, who was sexually abused as a child.

Despite these humiliating and de-humanizing experiences at the hands of staff, we are expected to work with them—no matter how they treat us—as we prepare for our release. We do not get to choose the officers who supervise us, nor the parole officers we must rely on for important documentation related to work, visits, and parole. After I began my process of change, I found this power imbalance frustrating as it often appeared that my case management team seemed to focus solely on the negative things about me. They did not give a lot of attention to all the good things I had done during my incarceration, including helping others.

Within the isolated environment of prison, there are many opportunities for corruption and abuses of power. Despite the increasing oversight as well as the growing reliance on security cameras, there are still many examples of correctional staff behaving badly towards inmates and one another. For example, on March 5, 2018, four staff from Edmonton Institution filed lawsuits against the prison and their own union claiming they were tortured, abused, and harassed.[3]

What happens inside prisons often transpires in secret. Abuse of power continues because of a lack of transparency, accountability, and the toxic nature of prison culture. Attempts to reduce contraband provide many opportunities for staff/inmate interactions that are anything but friendly. Common responses to suspected or actual threats to security are cell searches and lockdowns. This enhances mistrust and creates further barriers to rehabilitation and reintegration.

## *Lockdowns*

Lockdowns are not unusual in federal prisons and can last for days or even weeks. Often brought about by rumours or actual contraband or unrest,

3 https://globalnews.ca/news/4077943/edmonton-institution-lawsuit-torture-abuse-harassment/

lockdown means no showers, cold meals brought to your cell, and all work, activities, passes, and visits cancelled. Lockdowns are indefinite, so you have no idea how long you will be confined to your cell for 24 hr a day. If there is a cell search, you are removed from your cage and stripped searched. I have been strip searched more times over three decades than I could ever count. You would think I would have gotten used to this by now, but it doesn't get any easier. When you return to your cell, your belongings are everywhere and sometimes broken.

After having my cell tossed, I felt like a victim of a break and enter might. Knowing that everything I own has been touched and scrutinized by the officers left me with a sense of violation. It made it worse when the screws thanked me for my cooperation in the search. Like I ever had a choice in the matter.

## *Segregation*

Segregation, solitary confinement, or "the hole" was a big part of my prison experience. Today, it is a hotly debated topic especially due to the British Colombia superior court's decision in 2018 that segregation amounts to cruel and unusual punishment.

A prisoner can be placed in segregation for many reasons. It can be a means to punish someone who has violated prison regulations. Conversely, a prisoner can request time in segregation if they are feeling their personal safety is at risk due to outstanding debts or the nature of their offence. Prisoners can be put in segregation while they are being investigated by the CSC or by the authorities outside the institution. I have been placed in segregation during an investigation for illicit activity, participating in the underground economy, intimidating within the population, and traffic of influence, which meant that because of my status within the prison, when something criminal happened I was the first to blame. For example, once a prison labour strike started in protest of the living conditions within the institution. The strike started in the morning, and by 11:00 am, my brother, three other inmates, and myself were placed in segregation. We were accused of creating a climate of terror within the inmate population, and were, therefore, responsible for starting the strike. Although we had nothing to do with this strike, it was easy to blame and punish us due to our reputation.

Segregation is a prison within prison. Occupants are only allowed out for about one hour a day for a walk in a small, fenced yard, usually adjacent to the segregation cell. During "seg" time, there is usually no contact with anyone else. I cannot express how impactful total isolation is on the human mind. Whether it is days, weeks, or years, nobody can emerge from such an experience unaffected. I have chronic depression as the result of solitary confinement. This depression has led to self-destructive and antisocial behaviour, self-harm, and suicide attempts. While some of these mental health concerns came into prison with me, they got worse the longer I was there and the more time I spent isolated with only the torture of my own thoughts.

It was during these times of isolation I came to grips with the sad reality that I would never have the chance to start a family or participate in a meaningful career. I would not become a psychologist, a doctor, a firefighter, a lawyer, an engineer, or any other professional. I realized I had lost most of my social skills and had become afraid of groups of people I didn't know. Recognizing these dark truths in the company of only yourself is a devastating feeling. I changed so much I had trouble recognizing myself in the mirror. The years ran into each other, and although the world was changing outside, the inside stayed the same. One of the only sources of light through the darkness was access to meaningful work, education, and meeting others who gave me hope to better myself.

## Work & School

Every prisoner who is admitted to a federal institution is obligated to work. There are various posts available inside the prison walls such as maintenance, cleaning, and laundry. Some limited training is available for more specialized vocations (i.e. plumbing, mechanics) or you can participate in CORCAN industries. CORCAN is a special operating agency within CSC where prisoners can build employable skills. CORCAN offers third-party certified vocational training in areas including construction and trades. People working with CORCAN work on skills such as reliability, time management, and working with others.

Every prisoner in Canada receives a daily income. Those who do not participate in work programs but need to learn money management receive $1 per day. Those who work can receive more but pay tops out at $6.90 per day. The average Canadian prisoner receives $3 a day after deductions for room and board, mandatory savings, and phone administration. There are exemptions from paying room and board if you can demonstrate you are sending out your earnings to help your family.

With what is left, prisoners can buy things sold in the institution's canteen and order other items from a catalogue, such as clothes, shoes, radios, and TVs. It took a long time to save up for more expensive items and the price of goods kept increasing while our income stayed the same. While some people have family and friends who send them money, these sources dry up as the years pass. Most prisoners are not connected to people who have the resources to send much. According to a report by the CBC, despite inflation, Canadian prisoners have not had a pay raise in 32 years, even though the Correctional Service of Canada's own figures show the cost of items has risen more than 700%. Furthermore, inmates are now expected to use their pay to purchase items that the prison no longer provides, such as soap, shampoo, deodorant, stationery, and stamps.[4]

I had a Grade 6 education when I went into adult prison. I moved so frequently between schools that I had not benefitted academically or socially. In some schools, I only attended a week before my behaviour resulted in my immediate expulsion. In one school, even though I had not passed Grade 6, they placed me in Grade 8 saying I was too old to attend Grade 6. Being in Grade 8 when I was not ready made me feel stupid and worthless. So while I benefitted from some of the work programs inside, I appreciated educational opportunities even more. I was able to get some sense of pride and accomplishment in prison when I was able to complete 5 years of school in one. I worked on my studies in my cell and attended school for 1 hr a day, armed with my questions from the lessons. I refused to sit in school all day as this was where people went to "fuck the dog." Other prisoners would sit around,

4 https://www.cbc.ca/news/federal-inmates-go-on-strike-to-protest-pay-cuts-1.1875491

smoke, and chat, and this environment was not helpful for me to complete my studies.

It is well known that education helps support rehabilitation and this was definitely the case for me. Through hard work and determination, I earned a high school diploma and completed six college courses by correspondence. I also did Bible studies, a small business course, and finished programs for pest control, culinary arts, and construction. The advanced courses helped me see life in a new way and grow as a person.

Unfortunately, through my incarceration I saw the elimination of post-secondary education for prisoners. It was so frustrating to see life-changing programs taken away for political gain based on public pressure. The arguments against prison education and rehabilitation are so misguided. Citizens want safe communities but advocate for fewer programs and more punishment, which makes incarcerated people more dangerous. Currently, the only way to achieve higher education in prison is to find a course that does not rely on on-line submissions (we do not have access to the Internet) and pay for it yourself. Not easy with $3 a day when university courses cost hundreds of dollars.

## *Rehabilitation*

The correctional system in Canada claims to focus on rehabilitation which is defined as addressing the underlying needs and risks of prisoners to reduce the likelihood of re-offending. Even for people like me who wanted to change, it is very difficult to rehabilitate in the inherently oppressive and violent context of prison.

CSC has offered different programs over the years based on shifting criminological theories and research. I have seen many therapies come and go and have taken every program that was offered and relevant to me during my time inside. When the public reads that someone on parole committed a violent crime, it is natural that they have serious doubts about the rehabilitation process. I would agree that not everyone is interested in rehabilitation. This process is very personal as it means fighting against the desire to adapt to the prison environment and passively doing your time. Rehabilitation is active, on-going, and a lot of hard work. The hostile prison culture makes attempts at rehabilitation challenging because healing requires vulnerability and stark honesty. When others notice these traits in group therapy, you are at risk of manipulation. For this reason, many prisoners will not engage in therapy as most treatment programs take place in a group setting with individual assessment and follow up with a psychologist or a psychiatrist. I like to say that any healing I have done has been despite prison, not because of it.

CSC uses rehabilitation programs to reward prisoners by counting participation in them as points towards lowering security levels and increasing the likelihood of parole. Although CSC cannot mandate or force treatment, it certainly can coerce participation in prison programs. If you refuse programming, it is likely you will remain incarcerated.

Any sort of coercion gets in the way of true rehabilitation. If you have prisoners feeling forced to participate in a group, they will spend the entire session making noises and disturbing the rest. Then there are those who just play the game. They pretend to benefit from what is being taught and then use drugs in their cells at night. For those who want to be there, it is very difficult to derive benefit from the program no matter how good the content or facilitator is.

Due to my reputation in prison, when I decided to truly engage in rehabilitation programs, my friends supported me. I learned tools to help me keep thinking positively throughout my sentence. I discovered thinking errors that had caused a lot of damage in my life and was able to face some of the trauma of the past.

## *Prison Under the Influence*

I stopped doing drugs in 1997 and drinking alcohol in 2001. I quit cold turkey and will never go back. For those who are unable to do this, they need to find people that they can trust to support their decision to be sober. I had support from those around me to quit drugs and I am grateful for that.

The availability of substances in prison is a significant barrier to rehabilitation and a source of tremendous violence. Despite the best efforts of CSC to reduce contraband, drugs remain a serious issue for both staff and prisoners.

Some of the strategies used to deter drugs in prison are randomized urine tests. Those who refuse to give their urine for analysis are punished through fines, detention, loss of privileges, suspension of general visits, and Private Family Visits. On the other hand, some prisoners voluntarily provide urine samples. These volunteers are rewarded with good reports that can help lower their security levels.

Those of us who have consumed a lot of drugs easily understand that different substances stay in your system for differing amounts of time. Softer drugs like marijuana stay in your system for weeks compared to addictive substances like heroin which are only detectable in urine for two days following consumption. This reality has caused many people I know to pick up serious habits during their prison sentence. An altered state can be an enticing way to cope with the pains of imprisonment and boredom.

I sincerely believe that any form of rehabilitation must be done on a voluntary basis. Forcing someone to rehabilitate is a waste of time for everyone. I have seen people who I never thought would change suddenly make an effort. This should remind us that it is crucial to offer support and help once it is asked for. And to never give up.

## *The Loss of My Father: Pains of Imprisonment*

In addition to the daily indecencies of imprisonment, there are significant life events that occur that are excruciatingly painful. An example from my sentence was when I lost my father. The pain that piled onto the darkness I was already living in was almost unbearable at times; it demonstrates how loss can affect people in prison.

Although some people tell me I should have some hatred towards my father for abandoning us to the state after our mother died, I do not hate him. I believe that he loved all his children and imagine it must have been very difficult for him after his wife, our mother, died, and he was responsible for eight children. I believe many might have done the same thing in his shoes. In fact, I always had a lot of respect for my father. I do wonder what that respect was based on. Perhaps it was the fear of the unknown or the expectation that one *should* have respect for one's father.

As a child, I remember driving around with my father in his truck while he was delivering windows. He had a glass company in Ottawa called The City Glass Company. One day, a truck hit us on the passenger side where I was sitting. In those days, we really didn't care about seatbelts and I was sitting with my leg between the seat and the door. When the truck hit us, my leg got stuck. I remember this not because I was hurt, but because my father was pulling me from under my armpits and yelling. I was trying to tell him that my leg was stuck, and I needed to loosen it. This memory reminds me that my father tried to protect me when he could. There was no way he could have known the horrors I would experience in foster care. He was trying to do what was best for me.

My father died in 1988 when I was 26 years old and serving my third prison sentence. I used to call my father every 6 months or whenever I went back to prison. At the time of his death, I was in Joyceville Institution, a medium-security institution near Kingston, Ontario. My brother, Luc, was also in Ontario. He was locked up in Millhaven Institution, maximum-security. I just happened to call my father from Joyceville 1 week before he passed away. He was so sick that he couldn't talk, and my stepmother was doing most of the translation. I couldn't really understand anything that he or she was saying.

A week later, I got called to the chaplain's office and was told that my father had died. I called Luc and we decided that because he was in a maximum-security prison and I was in a medium with only 13 months left before being released on mandatory supervision, I had a better chance of going to the funeral service. I met with my case management team to request an Escorted Temporary Absence (ETA) to the village where my father's service would be held. The Classification Officer (today, they are called Institutional Parole Officers) explained that it would be a very expensive trip and she didn't think that the ETA would be accepted. I told her that I was willing to pay for the trip. She went back to talk to the people in charge but later that day informed me that the institution had denied my request. The lost opportunity to pay my respects to my father is one of the pains of imprisonment that many outside the walls will never know.

## *Love & Marriage*

Although I missed out on a lot of things that free citizens experienced, I was married and divorced in prison. My ex-wife, Carmen, and I met while I was in Donnacona Institution when one of her adult sons (who was incarcerated and on the same range) introduced us because his mother wanted to correspond with someone from the inside.

Our connection grew as Carmen started to visit me. After a few months, we decided to get married. Once we were married, the prison provided opportunities for Private Family Visits (PFV) where we could be alone together in a trailer on the prison grounds. Correctional officers would check on us from time to time.

One day near the end of October in 1999, I phoned Carmen to tell her the dates of our next PFV. She informed me that she could not handle this lifestyle anymore and wanted a divorce. I told Carmen that I understood and thanked her for the wonderful years and love that she had given me. I had 15 years left on my sentence, and she had been with me almost 6 years. I'm not saying that I wasn't hurting inside; however, there was no need to be egocentric. I reversed the roles and asked myself what I would have done in Carmen's situation. Had I been a free man with a wife serving a double life sentence for murder, I would have tried to hold on to her if I could. But I knew that sooner or later, I would have asked her for a divorce too. Carmen was not the one doing a life sentence, so why should she suffer as I was?

To be kept in captivity goes against the morality, logic, and nature of every human being and animal. Detention is a wound that never fully heals. As incarcerated people, we face problems that are physical, emotional, social, and psychological in nature. We are affected deeply by this hostile environment and these impacts last a lifetime. No matter how long your sentence is, captivity will never be normal for anyone. Prison impacts us as individuals and everyone we are connected to: wives, children, parents, siblings, parents, and friends. These impacts last a lifetime, particularly for those who are given a life sentence.

Prison sentences are meant to punish individuals while trying to rehabilitate them. When I consider the meaning and practice of "punishment" through incarceration, I find it interesting that prison aims to cause harm while expecting healing at the same time. Can you do both at once? The strongest message sent by punishment through captivity is one of retribution and vengeance. We claim to be civilized human beings, but we still sentence people to suffer.

Today, punishment does not involve physical torture but psychological torture. In my experience, psychological torture is a lot harder for a prisoner, because physical wounds can be usually heal over time. However, psychological wounds affect us the rest of our lives. People outside of prison can understand this as well as we all carry emotional scars on our soul. Life sentences, such as the one I am serving now, replaced capital punishment over 30 years ago. The following chapter outlines my views on the controversial subject of capital punishment.

# CHAPTER 4 - CAPITAL PUNISHMENT

Many people wiser than I am have written on this controversial subject. Victims of violence, families of offenders, lawyers, politicians, criminologists, and community members all participate in the debate. However, over the years I have noticed that perpetrators of violence like me are the least likely to be asked their views on capital punishment. Most opinions circulating about the abolition of capital punishment belong to politicians hoping to be elected or re-elected. Voices like mine are absent in public discourse about this topic and what I have to say may surprise many. My purpose is not to offend but to articulate a different opinion on an emotional topic. Although Canada has not allowed capital punishment for over 40 years, this subject remains emotionally, philosophically, and practically contentious.

Life sentences replaced capital punishment, which was abolished in Canada in 1976. People doing these sentences are called "lifers" and in 2013 we made up about 23% of the federal prison population. People serving a life sentence like me will be the property of the Correctional Service of Canada (CSC) until we die. A premeditated or first-degree murder results in an automatic life sentence with no possibility of parole for 25 years. Second-degree murder is killing that is intentional but not premeditated and parole eligibility can range from 10–25 years, depending on the circumstances and nature of the murder. Involuntary manslaughter sentences do not carry automatic life terms and vary greatly from 6 months in prison to life without parole for 10 years.

Given that I was sentenced to life in prison without parole for 25 years, I am serving the sentences I received afterwards concurrently. Being eligible for parole did not mean I was to be released automatically at 25 years. When this day came, I had to show the Parole Board of Canada (PBC) that, after decades in custody, I was a low risk to public safety. This was a tremendous challenge given my violent past and how institutionalized I had become within prison walls.

Once a prisoner has served the minimum number of years determined by their sentence, they have the right to present their case to the PBC. The PBC has the power to grant or refuse parole applications. I know several prisoners serving life sentences who were eligible for parole after 10 years, but they have been inside for 20 years. They have no idea when they will be released because, as a lifer, you can be kept inside prison until you are wheeled out in a body bag.

For lifers with a parole eligibility date of 15 years or more, we had one chance (besides winning an appeal) to be released before our eligibility date. Article 745.6 of the *Criminal Code* was known as the "Faint Hope Clause" and applied to anyone who committed a murder and received a life sentence before December 2, 2011. This meant that prisoners could apply to the Chief Judge of the province they were incarcerated in to reduce the period of the eligibility for release on parole. The judge then would appoint a Superior Court Judge who would oversee the formation of a 12-member jury to hear the case. Juries would hear evidence from police reports, victim impact statements, and psychological assessments. Their decision about changing the parole eligibility date would be based on the character of the prisoner, behaviour while in prison, the nature of the crime, and any other questions the judge considered relevant. The decision had to be unanimous or a new hearing would be called. If the prisoner did not like the decision, they could appeal to the Supreme Court of Canada.

The Faint Hope Clause was implemented when capital punishment was abolished to encourage rehabilitation and acknowledge that other countries allowed people convicted of murder to be paroled after an average of 15 years of incarceration. This clause aimed to provide prisoners with long sentences motivation to change through hope of liberation. This hope, however faint, was meant to reduce violence within prisons and promote transformation.

Despite its humanitarian intentions, the Faint Hope Clause drew significant negative attention from the media. When it appeared that serial murders such as Clifford Olson or Paul Bernardo could use this clause to gain early parole, the public raised hell, which caused politicians to react. In June of 1996, the Liberal government presented a bill which amended article 745 so that anyone who killed more than one person would not be eligible to apply. This bill was passed and later calls to "get tough on crime" resulted in the Faint Hope Clause being removed completely from the *Criminal Code* in March of 2011.

There are many reasons the world should be afraid of monsters like Paul Bernardo, and I understand that concern. However, it is unlikely that men like this would ever be able to persuade a jury of 12 people that the progress they have made in prison over 15 years is enough to warrant early release. It is impossible for me to imagine that someone who has committed such heinous crimes against women and children would be able to demonstrate they are no longer a threat and deserve reintegration. Even if the jury did grant this, the prisoner would still have to apply to the PBC for release, which is never guaranteed.

Despite these checks and balances, public misunderstanding and fear ultimately resulted in all lifers losing the chance for early parole. Removing hope reduces our desire to change and increases the risk of violence. When the Faint Hope Clause was removed, I saw firsthand the intensified violence in prisons between prisoners and towards staff. While the removal of capital punishment and introduction of life sentences was meant to be a progression towards the more humane treatment of prisoners, I have observed and experienced intense psychological torture. Rather than a quick death by lethal injection, the process of killing now extends over decades.

People who oppose capital punishment often will say, "If you are not executed, you have a chance to have your freedom one day." But I will never be free. If capital punishment is physical death, a life sentence is mental and social death.

My life sentence was not my first time in custody. My mother died when I was 5 years old and I was placed in foster homes where I was neglected and physically, emotionally, and sexually abused. When I went to a youth custody centre when I was 11, I felt safe. I have been in institutions most of my life since then. What kind of a man have I become after being in captivity for close to 32 years as an adult?

Is it crueller to keep a man in a concrete box for 25 years or to give him a lethal injection that will end his life? Those who would say any life is better than death cannot conceive of what it is like to be locked up for a long period of time. The psychological impacts of incarceration are torturous for both humans and animals. It is not only the daily indignities of prison life, but the long-term impacts that prevent both humans and animals from returning to flourish in their natural habitat.

Suppose we can agree that long periods of incarceration are equivalent to psychological torture. In that case, some may argue that this is a natural result of the choice to commit murder. I agree. I cannot deny this. I will never forget the acts of violence I used. I think about them every day and will for the rest of my life. I cannot forget the evil things that I have done to my victims and their loved ones. I am not the only one who will never forget. Anytime I started to try and improve my self-worth in prison, people working there seemed to take great pleasure in reminding me of all that I have done. I was never judged for the positive steps I was taking, but only for the horrors of my past.

My history both defined me and protected me from the abuse of others. Because violence served me, it was difficult to choose a path towards change or a future without violence. At a young age, I learned that the best way to stop people from abusing you is to have them fear you. As a result, it was hard to let violence go.

Long prison sentences demonstrate the cruelty society can inflict when they do not see the consequences up close. Nobody but the prisoner truly witnesses the slow death within the tortured mind. I took someone's life in minutes; mine is being taken over a lifetime. My suffering is drawn out over hours, days, weeks, years, and decades. I am not saying my act of life-taking is any better or more ethical than the life sentence I am serving. Killing will almost always be wrong. But suffering, too, is almost always wrong. When a horse has a broken leg, we do not let that animal suffer more than it must. The horse would be euthanized to end its suffering. Even a vicious dog who bites someone will be euthanized, not kept in a cage for the rest of its life.

Even though I was released from prison, the knowledge that my sentence will never end crushes me like a weight. Until I die a natural death, the government will have power over everything I do and could, at any time, bring me back into prison. They don't need a reason.

Some members of the public will argue for capital punishment because they believe prisoners cost taxpayers too much money. We are supervised in and outside of prison for decades, which costs millions, and the conditions are "too good" for the likes of us.

Our cells are too well furnished, we have TVs, and three meals a day. Most people who claim prisoners have too much have never spent a night inside of a prison. It is true that prison and parole costs taxpayers billions of dollars every year in Canada. So, what is life like inside?

I have spent time in many different institutions and not every cell is the same. Older prisons have "open cells" where the door is a set of bars. Newer institutions have steel doors and minimum-security prisons have rooms with regular doors, not cells.

An average cell in a Canadian federal institution is 12' x 8' and contains a desk, sink, toilet, locker, chair, and bed. These are the only items, besides bedding and institutional clothing, that are provided and paid for with taxpayers' money. "Items I have possessed over the years include a 14" flat-screen colour television, a selection of cassettes and compact disks, a Walkman, an alarm clock, desk lamp, books, sandals, cups, personal papers, photos albums, letters, cards, and legal documents. I also had materials for my hobbies, which included cross-stitch and model ship building. All these I purchased myself with the few dollars a day I made by working in prison

All the material possessions I had in the world fit in a cell where I also slept, ate, studied, relaxed, and took care of personal grooming. I spent an average of 16 hours in those cells for decades, depending on the level of security. The higher the level of security the more time you are locked up in your cage.

If you still think that we have it too good in prison, try this experiment. At home, lock yourself in your bathroom with any item you think would make this more comfortable. Take anything you want: television, stereo, video game, all the food you can eat, your computer or phone, books. The only rule is, that once you are inside and close the door, you cannot open it yourself.

It may sound fun or even relaxing to spend some time alone with your possessions. However, at some point, you will have had enough. Imagine not being able to leave for days, weeks, or years. Now imagine you cannot have any communication devices, so you are cut off completely from the outside world.

So, if long sentences get in the way of rehabilitation, are extremely expensive, create more violence, and are cruel, why do we still use them? How much punishment is enough and who gets to decide? I don't think any amount of punishment will redeem someone who has taken a life. Punishment doesn't bring the person who died back nor is it guaranteed to help victims with their healing. No matter what punishment is imposed, the self-hate and disgust within one's own heart and mind will exist. So, should we bring back capital punishment? I, and many other lifers, would say yes.

Every day, each one of us has a choice about whether to stay alive or to end things. Suicide is an option that most humans have. After getting sentenced to life, I considered suicide many times. I still consider it. When I was given my first life sentence, I wish I could have had an option: lethal injection or a life 25 sentence. I know I would have chosen death over life in prison. I don't consider this suicide but pragmatic euthanasia. Committing suicide in prison is difficult and messy. Many do not succeed—as there are insufficient means available—so we are left in padded cells on suicide watch. Mercy killing is now a legal practice in Canada that aims to release an individual from intolerable suffering caused by disease. The disease I suffer from is post-traumatic stress disorder based on years of abuse in foster homes. I acquired the "disease" of institutionalization, which I will live with until the day I die. The impacts of long-term incarceration will never go away. I consider capital punishment as euthanasia for people in prison.

Had I been given the choice of euthanasia upon sentencing, my death would have saved taxpayers millions of dollars. Based on the costs estimated by the Parliamentary Budget Officer (PBO) in 2016–2017, my time in prison alone amounts to over three million dollars. I spent approximately 9 years in minimum ($47,370 or $130 per day), 11.5 years in medium-security ($75,077 or $206 per day), 9.5 years in maximum-security ($92,740 or $254 per day), and 2 years total in segregation ($463,045 per year).

Parole costs about $18,000 a year and will continue to add up as I will be supervised in the community until I die. If I live another 20 years, you can add another half a million to the cost of my life sentence.

Where else could that money have been spent? How many people could that have helped? My victims would not have gotten a fraction of that money for assistance. In our system, over 95% of the resources go to locating, prosecuting, and supervising offenders. The average tuition costs for one post-secondary student in Canada is a little over $20,000. The average cost of a federal prisoner is equivalent to five students attending university for a year.

I would not consider my death cruel and inhumane treatment; rather, liberation for my victims and the state. I no longer cost taxpayers, nor am I painful to my victims' loved ones. To keep a human being in long-term captivity is an act of cruelty, and I am not alone in this feeling. I did some research to prove it.

About 12 years into my sentence, I had started to change my life. I was taking a Sociology course by correspondence that I paid for myself (post-secondary education in prison was removed in the 1990s). One of the course assignments was aimed at assessing my knowledge of research methods. I looked at the list of the suggested topics but couldn't relate to any of them, so I contacted the professor and asked if I could do research on capital punishment within prison. The professor agreed that this would be an interesting project and I used what I learned in the course to create a questionnaire. Using the respect and reputation I had in prison, I went from cell to cell asking lifers if they would participate, and most were happy to complete the anonymous survey. I asked, "Knowing what you now know about doing a life sentence, would you have chosen lethal injection over a life sentence?" While they were clear they wouldn't want the death penalty imposed, 98% said they would have chosen the option of a quick death.

This affirmed my own experience that when you get a life sentence, at some point, you realize that if you do not take accountability for your actions and your life, you will never get out. With accountability comes depression as you face the harm you have done to so many, including yourself. You experience grief and loss as you distance yourself from the criminal elements of prison culture. Now you are more isolated, full of shame and regret, and it becomes even more difficult to do time. As you look at the years still stretched out in front of you, your sense of self-worth depletes even further. Not everyone gets to a point of taking accountability for their actions, but the lifers who do suffer more than those who live in denial and adapt to prison's subculture.

Although I have argued against life sentences, I believe some prison time is necessary for some people. A time out, if you will. Some months or years in prison often can provide a much-needed opportunity to reflect on your life and what led you to cause someone else grievous harm. However, prisons are oppressive places. Instead of thinking about the people we have hurt, we often spend more time feeling like victims ourselves from the lack of health care, constant threat of violence, drugs, abuse from staff, isolation, and loneliness. This perpetual state of suffering can prevent us from dealing with our past hurts and having empathy for those we have hurt.

So, what should replace life without parole for 15 or 25 years? I believe in life sentences as most of us who have committed murder have backgrounds and experiences that mean we will require lifelong support. Trauma never disappears but is something I must live with each day. The community parole supervision that comes with a life sentence allows people with horrific backgrounds like mine to have access to housing, psychiatric services, and community support and accountability. However, parole eligibility should never be more than 10 years for any crime, even murder. Ten years provides sufficient time to rehabilitate without removing the hope that motivates change. Release after 10 years would not be automatic as one should have to demonstrate they are working on themselves, and help must be available for them to do so. Those unwilling to engage in rehabilitation would have the right to end their lives through capital punishment.

When I tell people I would have chosen death over a life sentence they say, "But if you had made that choice, you wouldn't be alive to have this conversation! Look at all you have accomplished since you have been out." I reply, "Had I chosen for my life to be over after my first life sentence, my second victim would still be alive." I would have given my life to avoid all the future victims I created.

The public's fear of people in prison is driven by misunderstanding and assumptions. We, in prison, are the "other" and the other is feared. But not everyone incarcerated for murder are the same. Ask our partners, brothers, sisters, parents, grandparents, co-workers, and everyone who has had the chance to know us. One of the only things that lifers have in common is that someone has died because of our actions. So, are we all dangerous beasts who are incapable of rehabilitation?

It may surprise many people to know that most people serving life for murder will never kill again. And this isn't because we are locked up forever. In fact, 99% of all lifers will be released on parole eventually. According to data about paroled lifers from the Parole Board of Canada, 13% breached their parole conditions, 6% committed non-violent offences, and 3% committed violent offences. Lifers have the lowest rate of re-offending compared to all other prisoners, including sexual offenders.

Personal transformation happens in prison. I know because it happened to me. At one time, I was considered a very dangerous individual and locked away for 20–23 hours a day in a super-maximum institution. In 2020, I celebrated 7 years on parole, and I have not used violence in over 20 years. Like me, there are many others who are locked up who have changed and have much to contribute to society. But all of us change despite the slow mental and social death associated with long term incarceration. With the support of caring of volunteers and our own resilience, we are able to exist. Most of the time, it is not much of a life, but I try my best to make the most of the fact I am still here. I am an avid community volunteer and parishioner. I am a provider, loving husband, caring grandfather, and a good friend.

The psychological effects of long-term incarceration seem to be misunderstood and ignored by those who oppose the death penalty in favour of life sentences. I came into prison as a young man and watched my hair and beard turn from brown to grey to white. I stopped recognizing the man in the mirror. Every day I wake up, I think about the years wasted inside those prison walls and all those people I hurt. The depression kicks in once again, and it is often a struggle to find the will to stay alive. It would have been much easier to stay inside and die there than to face the hurdles in the community that institutionalization brings.

*Yves and his brother, Luc. Donnacona Institution, maximum-security.*
*Near Quebec City, Quebec, 1994.*

*Yves, Donnacona Institution, maximum-security. Near Quebec City, Quebec, 1994.*

*Yves, Special Handling Unit (Supermax). Prince Albert, Saskatchewan, 1996.*

*Yves' cell in Atlantic Institution, maximum-security. Renous, New Brunswick, 1997.*

*Yves squatting 600 lb in a weight competition at Le Clerc Institution, medium-security. Laval, Quebec, 2001.*

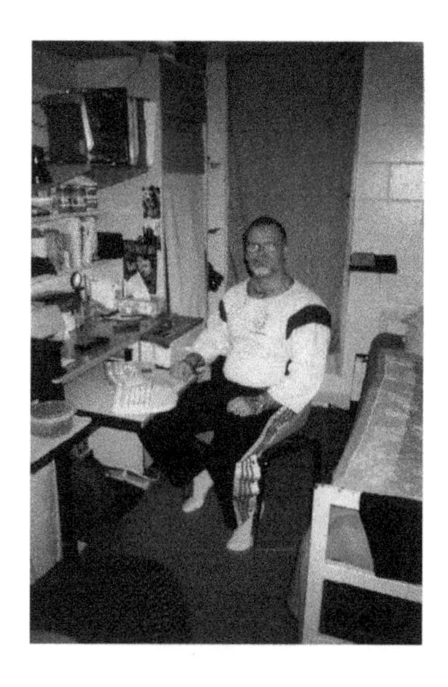

*Yves' cell in La Macaza, medium-security. Near Mount Tremblant, Quebec, 2002.*

*Yves and Luc, Mission Institution, medium-security. In 32 years, Luc was the only biological family member to visit Yves in federal prison. Mission, British Columbia, 2004.*

*Yves holding a ship he built as one of his hobbies. Mission Institution, medium-security. Mission, British Columbia, 2004.*

*Yves holding a ship he built as one of his hobbies. Mission Institution, medium-security. Mission, British Columbia, 2004.*

*Yves posing in the gym in Mission Institution, medium-security. Mission, British Columbia, 2005.*

*Yves and a very close friend and brother in Christ, Robert. Yves considers Robert an exceptional human being that helped grow his faith. They are seated next to a petit point of the Mona Lisa that took Yves 1500 hours to complete. Petit point is a form of canvas embroidery similar to cross-stitch embroidery, but even finer due to it small scale. Yves took up petit point as a hobby while in prison and completed 20 different pieces.*

*The first job Yves got upon release from prison. Chilliwack, British Columbia, 2013.*

*Yves' very first car gifted to him by a very close friend after receiving day parole. Chilliwack Community Corrections Centre. Chilliwack, British Columbia, 2014.*

*Yves at one of his first jobs as a prep-cook/carver in a hotel restaurant. Chilliwack, British Columbia, 2015.*

*Yves serving Sunday brunch. Chilliwack, British Columbia, 2015.*

*Yves and his beautiful, loving wife Kim. Chilliwack, British Columbia, 2015.*

*Working as a prep cook. Chilliwack, British Columbia, 2015.*

*Yves was humbled to be invited as one of the speakers for a conference attended by survivors of homicide. Vancouver area, British Columbia, 2016.*

*Yves and his Harley Davidson Sportster 1200. Chilliwack, British Columbia, 2018.*

*Yves at his current job in a plastic factory. Fraser-Valley, British Columbia, 2020.*

*Yves, his wife, Kim, and Yves' stepson, Morgan, at Morgan's high school graduation. Chilliwack, British Columbia, 2018.*

*Yves outside a provincial jail about to go back into prison to facilitate an Alternatives to Violence Project workshop for some of the residents. Lower Mainland, British Columbia, 2019.*

# CHAPTER 5 - THE AWAKENING

Yves' history is comprised of many traumas. According to the American Psychological Association, trauma is an emotional response to a terrible event like an accident, rape, or natural disaster. Immediately after the event, shock and denial are typical. Longer term reactions include unpredictable emotions, flashbacks, strained relationships, and even physical symptoms like headaches or nausea.

For those who experience trauma, some will develop post-traumatic stress disorder (PTSD), which involves persistent, intense, and disturbing thoughts and feelings related to the traumatic event. Those who suffer with PTSD may relive the event through flashbacks or nightmares; feel sadness, shame, fear, or anger; and experience detachment or estrangement from other people. People with PTSD may avoid situations or people that remind them of the traumatic event and could have strong negative reactions to something as ordinary as a loud noise or an accidental touch.

In Canada, PTSD rates range from 1.1%–3.5% amongst the general public. Those rates are 4%–32% for men in prison and it is well documented that incarceration makes PTSD symptoms worse (Baranyi, Cassidy, Fazel, Priebe, & Mundt, 2018). Over 35% of correctional staff meet the criteria for PTSD,[5] which means many traumatized people are responsible for the safety and security of other traumatized people. Although CSC psychiatrists will make PTSD diagnoses, very few programs exist to deal effectively with the source of the trauma. Rather, symptoms are "managed" through cognitive behavioural therapy and medications.

In addition to having higher rates of trauma and PTSD, most people in custody have experienced substantial adverse events in childhood, such as witnessing family violence, having 1 or more parents absent, or being involved with the child welfare system. At least half report a history of childhood physical, sexual, or emotional abuse and 15% to 20% of Indigenous persons in federal prisons have attended residential schools (Kouyoumdjian, Schuler, Matheson, & Hwang, 2016, p. 215). Compared to the general population, people in prison have much higher rates of brain injuries and mental illness. The majority of prisoners come from extremely disadvantaged backgrounds (poor or homeless, under-educated or illiterate, chronically under- or unemployed, oppressed through colonization and/or racism, have poor physical and mental health, often addicted to alcohol or other drugs). These biological, psychological, social and economic factors mean that many of the individuals locked up are marginalized and impoverished in mind, body, and spirit. The complexities of these challenges combined with the traumatizing effects of incarceration make transformation difficult. Although corrections in Canada currently utilize a "risk management" approach, promising advances in trauma-informed care may offer more hope for rehabilitation and healing. By focusing on resilience rather than deficits, people in prison can redefine themselves.

Trauma-informed services take into account an understanding of trauma in all aspects of service delivery and place priority on the individual's safety, choice, and control. Such services create a treatment culture of nonviolence, learning, and collaboration. The focus of interventions in prison should be to create emotional and physical safety and facilitate voice and choice in the healing process.

---

5 https://www.cbc.ca/news/canada/manitoba/stony-mountain-james-bloomfield-workers-compensation-corrections-canada-1.5110580

Although research and practice demonstrate the positive impact of trauma-informed care, correctional systems in Canada have a very long way to go to change how people doing time and staff are treated. While rehabilitation is the stated priority of corrections, the reality of what is actually possible within an inherently punitive and traumatizing environment like a prison is much different. While serious and radical reform is needed now, we must not lose sight of a future world without prisons. In this future, those who must be separated from society must be cared for within re-imagined spaces where they are treated with the human dignity and compassion mostly absent in institutions today.

My journey to transforming my life began with an experience I call "the awakening." This event was triggered when I hit rock bottom after receiving a second life sentence for the 1993 murder of another prisoner. It was almost Christmas in 1995, and I had been transferred from Donnacona, a maximum-security prison, to Quebec's Special Handling Unit (SHU). The SHU is known to house "the worst of the worst" of Canada's prisoners. Most of the population is comprised of people transferred from maximum-security institutions who have been involved in serious incidents and cannot be managed under normal security.

I was alone in my cell remembering that the last Christmas I spent out of prison was in 1981. Over more than 10 years, I had grown accustomed to spending the holidays inside. We prisoners say that we don't care about Christmas; it was just another day and we would go about our routine. But if we were honest, we would say that Christmas was a particularly hard time. We were missing out on being with our loved ones and sharing the joy of the holidays, gifts, food, and drink. Although we didn't talk about it, we grieved the fact that we were not part of celebrations during the holiday season.

So, I am in segregation, have nothing in my cell, it is dark and cold outside, I have just received a second life sentence, and it's Christmas. I have been totally cut off from everyone, including my wife at the time. People in prison often can be heard saying that the only life sentence that really counts is the first one—the rest are all free. Most people who say this are not doing life. As a lifer myself, I will tell you that after receiving a second life sentence, I felt I had only dug myself deeper into a pit of hopelessness. As I looked at the barred window, I could see my reflection in the glass. For a moment, I could see the reflection of my father standing there, looking at me. My heart became heavy and I started to pray. I didn't have anywhere else to turn, so as I prayed, I was given the chance to look deeply into my soul.

I had always said, I don't care what happens to me. My life isn't worth anything. However, during that prayer I looked back at my life with the knowledge that the person in the cell next to mine was my younger brother, Luc. My heart ached knowing that I was responsible for him being in the SHU with me. I was the one responsible for the murder in Donnacona and if it wasn't for me, Luc would have never been involved. This moment sparked the deep realization that something had to change.

The awakening I had in that naked cell began a process of transformation that continues to this day. The experience in that solitary place made me realize I had been wrong most of my life and that I would have to live with the consequences for the rest of it. Thinking of my brother next door and having empathy for him was a catalyst for my change. No longer was I thinking of only myself.

I was originally very hesitant to write about religion in this book. I actually removed much of my thoughts on this topic but later had a change of heart. I did this because I followed the advice from a friend that I should write about things I know. I know a great deal about religion and my faith has been central to my personal transformation. Decades later, my faith and faith community continue to be a vital part of my life.

I have been praying every day since that night in the SHU. At the time, I did not share my commitment to my faith with Luc or anyone else. I had been in prison a very long time and I have seen a lot of men become "federal Christians" just to try and get something out of it, only to walk away from the church once they had benefitted by the charade. For me, prayer had always been a personal thing. I never wanted to use Christianity or my faith to get what I wanted.

How people see me matters. I don't want to be seen as someone who manipulates others or the system. My personal integrity is very important to me. I share my views on religion as I want to be honest about who I am. Many people, however, have a problem with organized religion. This includes people in prison as they are constantly challenging the authorities that control all aspects of their daily lives and imposing rules and schedules. I understand this frustration and believe you can't impose your beliefs and values on others. Even if you use force or threat, what is imposed will not last. All you can do is share your ideas with others and hope they understand. There is a fine line between imposing and teaching, and this is a big problem when it comes to religion.

Religion and my faith community have helped me create a new identity—they inspired me to become someone not only known for violence, robberies, and harm. I wanted to be known for the love I have for God. I wanted to be known as the man God created me to be in the first place. I wanted to be known as a success story of a man who turned his life around and is a loving Christian who wants to help other people avoid making the same mistakes. I aimed to be a man who cares about others, who is loving, trustworthy, and helpful, and this is who I became.

## *Transforming: The Role of Empathy*

In addition to my faith, developing empathy for myself and others played a significant role in my transformation. It was something I had to re-learn because I had shut off my emotions long ago. I practiced empathy by reversing roles, putting myself in another's position. Through this mental exercise, I was able to better understand both those who victimized me and those I victimized. When thinking about my abusers in foster care, I realized I was an easy target for sexual predators because of my vulnerability. Imagining myself as that small, lost child helped me understand that I was not weak or to blame for these abuses. Trying to put myself in my father's shoes after losing my mother helped me understand my family situation better. I am not justifying or excusing other people's actions but rather trying to understand why people act as they do. This pursuit of understanding does not mean that everything is OK, but it does help avoid future pain by gaining perspective on how our actions impact others.

During psychological therapy in prison, I was asked to engage deeply with life events that have disturbed me the most. One such incident that arose powerfully was remembering 9/11. In considering this horrific event in a therapeutic session, I suddenly understood everything. I felt intense empathy as I considered that those killed in the towers of the World Trade Center and the first responders who died during the rescue. I considered the pain of this event rippling out to families, coworkers, and friends. Although this perspective would be second nature to most people, I was so detached from the experience of being human that this was something I had to learn. I had spent much of my life ignoring the suffering of others.

To commit a premeditated murder, you must be emotionally shut off. Murder is a completely egocentric act that involves thinking only of the self and never about the victims in the chain reaction that will follow. In the moment of a murder, I was not thinking about tomorrow. Murder is a double-edged sword. By killing someone, I killed many parts of myself as well. I executed the parts of me that might help build a family or a successful career. I eliminated the potential for a healthy social life—who would want to associate with a murderer who spent decades locked up?

Often, I relive the murders in my head. The scenes replay every time there is a victim of violence on the news. I cannot help remembering that I also have committed cruel acts that created so much sadness for my victims' loved ones. This is pain that I would not wish on anybody. I want to reassure my victims' families that I think about them much more often than they might think I do. My ability to share in another's emotions, thoughts, or feelings by empathizing and identifying with their needs and pain has softened my heart. It is more painful to experience empathy than being shut off; however, I cannot imagine anyone changing their evil ways without being able to put themselves in another's shoes.

For years, I believed my murders were justified. I compared my behaviour with that of a soldier or an executioner. My victims were criminals, so I was able to deny that I was really harming anyone.

In addition to considering my victims "lowlifes" like me, my motivations for using violence stemmed from the search for self-confidence I have been on since childhood. For the longest time, I thought that by looking strong and mean, being covered with tattoos, and using extreme violence I would be able to feel good about myself. However, it never worked. The bigger and more violent I got, the more scared I was, so the walls I built around me got higher. I wanted to push people away so that they couldn't hurt me. As an adult, I was never concerned about physical violence but constantly feared emotional abuse from others.

I have sometimes felt envy for people found guilty of murder under the influence of drugs or alcohol or those who kill as a crime of passion. In my mind, they had an explanation for their actions. These factors are not an excuse, but it helps make their behaviour more understandable than my cold-blooded, calculated actions were.

Over the years, I have asked myself, "How would I react if somebody murdered my brother, Luc?" I know it would be the most heartbreaking day of my life. I ask myself a follow-up question, "What if this person's motivation for killing Luc was the same motivation I claimed for taking the lives of my victims?" The thought of someone taking my brother's life for such egocentric and selfish reasons created such extreme sadness. I could not think of any reason that the killer could give that would allow me to walk away and say, "OK, cool." This realization destroyed every excuse I ever made to try and justify my choices to use violence.

Empathy for those I have harmed has replaced the distorted thinking that fuelled my violence. When I think about all the people I have hurt, I feel deep sadness, depression, regret, remorse, and a sense of failure. I often say to people who apologize to me that "sorry" doesn't mean anything if they don't change their behaviour. So as remorseful as I am for my actions, it does not mean anything if I do not fulfill my commitment to living a life of non-violence. Through the practice of empathy and taking responsibility for my actions, I can honestly say I had only two incidents that involved violence since 1995. These occurred in 1999 and there were only minor injuries as I was able to use my skills and deescalate the potential for extreme violence.

Moving away from using violence is also difficult because I struggle with self-loathing. I live with the knowledge that my behaviour destroyed human lives and the lives of my victim's family members and friends. My actions went beyond stealing or breaking something and have consequences that can never be undone. While my punishment is measured by years in prison and on parole, I feel that my real sentence is living with the knowledge of my actions for the rest of my life. My sentence involves sitting with the regret that I had the choice to back off and chose not to. My sentence is knowing that I am the only one responsible for my actions. I have bitterness toward people who hurt me in the past, but there has never been anybody who has hurt me as much as I have hurt myself. How can one be able to love or forgive a human being so destructive?

It was through my faith and development of empathy that my transformation began. How do I know that God has answered my prayers? Today, I see evidence everywhere. I have authentically taken responsibility for my actions and committed to making change. I am living in the community on parole and have turned my life around. I have let go of drugs, alcohol, and violence. I am respected for who I am today and not for the violence I have used in the past. I understand that respect earned though violence is only good as long as you keep using violence. Respect earned though loving actions will last a lifetime.

Yves' healing journey began as an internal process in a segregation cell and continued as a result of work he did within the context of a caring community of support. Despite rehabilitation being a stated goal of corrections, prison often impedes healing and change through its oppressive structure. Rehabilitation, also known as re-entry, resettlement, reintegration, recovery, desistence, is based on the legal notion of therapeutic jurisprudence where the focus of legal interventions should be on addressing the social problems that lead to offending, not punishment. However, being subjected to lockdowns, loneliness, strip searches, cell extractions, substances, the threat of violence, and other indignities will be experienced as punitive, no matter what the intent.

White & Graham (2014) note that justice as rehabilitation practice in corrections should be based on four propositions:

- Justice ought to be an active process
- Justice is about maximizing liberty
- Justice deals with the whole person
- Justice must look back, be in the present, and look forward

These elements can be found in Yves' justice journey. Although living in environments where his liberty was minimized, he became an active agent of his own personal transformation. Yves has experienced holistic change—mental, physical, emotional, relational, and spiritual. Like many formerly incarcerated people, he has learned how to live with the impacts of past trauma, cope in the present in a healthy way, and find hope for the future.

# CHAPTER 6 - MAKING CHANGES

This chapter relates to the journey I am on from being a violent person to a kind, non-violent person. Although the event of the awakening was the catalyst to this change, the process of transformation is an on-going one. Some of these changes have been very difficult and I have let go of some of the values that I had in the past. I had to step out of my comfort zone, look at myself in the mirror and ask, "Who are you and who do you really want to be?" For me, change has meant facing your past to see where you went wrong. This was painful as I had to realize the pain I have caused others. During the process of making change, I often found it hard to see anything good in me and hold onto it.

Although I have been inside the "correctional system" where the main goal is to change me, I have learned that change must be made of your own free will. Changes that are imposed will not last. Although being isolated from most of society provided me opportunities to change who I am, much of the hard work I have done on my own has been with the support of friends from the inside and outside. Other prisoners, chaplains and clerical staff, and community volunteers who saw beyond my actions gave me hope that my life could be different. I did not have to define myself by what I had done in the past.

In making change, the first thing I had to understand was the *process* of change. I learned a model of change while participating in the Violence

Prevention Program (VPP) in prison. The process of change was explained as a map that consisted of answering the following questions:

1. Is there a problem?
2. What is the problem?
3. Do I want to solve the problem?
4. When and how will I solve the problem?
5. Do I need help?
6. What kind of help?

I had to ask myself what was going wrong in my life that needed to be changed. It was easy to find the answer as there was so much in my life that I was not happy with. I had to ask myself,

What do I, Yves, need to change?

Do I, Yves, want to change?

Why do I, Yves, want to change?

Is there a problem?

Yes. I have been in prison for most of my adult life. I have trouble communicating with people. I feel that people around me fear me.

Why do I want to change?

I don't want to spend the rest of my life in prison. I do not want people to fear me. I want people to see me as a good communicator and a pro-social individual. I want people to accept me for my potential to help others, not for my potential to use extreme violence.

What do I need to change?

I need to change from the inside out. I need to shed the persona of someone to be feared. It wasn't just other scared convicts that steered clear of me. Institutional staff and volunteers that came to prison for chapel, social and self-employment activities also approached me with caution. When I first came to prison, I wanted others to fear me. Fear is a powerful protection and defence mechanism. For many years, it pleased me to see people afraid.

In the past, I was accepted and respected through fear of my potential for violence. Most of my life, I used instrumental violence and intimidation to keep people away from me or to get what I wanted from them. Violence is a powerful tool because, quite simply, it works. This is especially true in a prison context where the more violent you are, the more "respect" you are afforded. For example, I was given reverence from the prison population before people even met me due to my sentence of life in prison for first-degree murder. The more violence one used in the community, the greater social power one has inside prison. This aspect of the prison subculture is backwards from mainstream society where most forms of physical violence are frowned upon. In changing myself, I lost two of my most reliable and effective attributes in dealing with people: intimidation and violence. Abandoning these qualities would be risky for most prisoners but thankfully I received support for these changes from others.

Although I know living a non-violent life is the right thing to do, the process of change continues to bring me in and out of a depressed state of mind. As I am now honest with myself, am constantly exposed to the darkness inside me that made me act in violent ways. I feel the loss of all the time I have wasted behind my mask of insecurities. The depression kicks in when I realize that I have not only wasted other people's lives, but my own. At first, I blamed others for my actions: "My foster parents should have shown me love when I was a child instead of abusing me." Blaming others is always easier than taking responsibility for your own actions.

Let's look closer at what I call the "blame game." As a child, I did not have much control over my life. I experienced physical, verbal, and sexual abuse at the hands of adults. These memories bring anger. I feel it now as I write this and think back on how some people treated me. How my screams for help were not heard by anyone. Tears of rage flow as I think of how scared I was as a very small child. Instead of being loved, I was abused by those who were supposed to take care of my most basic needs. I blame them for my loss of self-esteem, self-confidence, faith in human kind, and trust in people. The last thing that I want to do is portray myself as a victim, but it is clear to me that hurt people hurt people.

In reflecting on my childhood hurts, I came to further realize the hurt I caused others. At certain times in my life, the only one responsible for my actions has been me. No one forced me to kill anyone, to pull the trigger six times, to stab a man many times. No one ever forced me to use that violence. I am the only one responsible for those actions. These thoughts create tremendous self-blame and depression as I realize I ruined my life more than anyone else ever could have. To make things worse, how many lives have my actions ruined? The depression deepens as I consider the ripple effect of my violence.

To change from a man of extreme violence to one of love and compassion, the best tool that I have used is the "third person perspective." I have asked myself, "How do people see you?" It is like watching a movie where you are the main character. By doing this, I could imagine how other people saw me. I did not like who I saw. I could understand why people feared me and did not want to approach me. I found that although understanding the process of change through the VPP was helpful, true change is not something you learn only in books or programs. You live it one day at a time. This is the process of change that I experienced and continue to this day.

In making change, I realized I had to change the way that I looked (physical appearance), my approach (social skills), and my attitude towards people (my view of others). As someone who spent a great deal of time in the weight pit, I have a related metaphor for change. When you first start working out with weights, the pain is almost unbearable. Over time, it gets less and less painful, and you start to see changes in your thoughts, feelings, and behaviour. The same goes for making other changes in your life. It is very painful at the start to take stock and discover all the parts of yourself that need work. The more changes you need to make, the more pain one will suffer. I had to change almost everything about myself if I was going to be successful in living a non-violent life.

The difference between spending lots of time in the weight pit and making changes towards non-violence is that the former commitment was never about being healthy. The goal of lifting heavy weights was to appear the biggest, strongest, and most intimidating as possible. In pursuing this goal, I became stronger than I could ever imagine bench pressing 350 lb, squatting 600, and deadlifting 540. After awakening to the impacts of my violence, weight lifting lost all purpose for me. I no longer wanted to use working out to intimidate anyone. I started thinking about physical activity as a way to stay healthy. This transformed my relationship with the gym as well as changing my physical look. I am still big and strong, but I am no longer the biggest or strongest, and I try and walk in a way that is not likely to be perceived as a challenge to others.

Making changes in my life involved other physical modifications. I used to shave my head, have a goatee, and wear dark sunglasses day and night. I did this in prison for about 8 years. Sometimes I would watch TV in my cell with no lights on wearing my sunglasses. What a sight that must have been for the officers doing their rounds. Today, I've grown my hair back—and it was quite a surprise to see it had changed colour from brown to, well, white! I shaved my goatee and left a small moustache. I have contact lenses now and only wear sunglasses when the sun is out.

I try to smile around people and avoid having the pissed off look that I perfected in prison to keep people away. My tattoos I will have to keep, but given their current popularity, I think I fit in just fine. When I was growing up the only people who had tattoos were sailors, veterans, bikers, and convicts. How the world has changed.

Changing your physical appearance can be easier than changing what is inside. Throughout my experience of change, I have been afraid. Scared of people calling me stupid, telling me to shut up, and putting me down in front of others. I don't know who said, "Sticks and stones can break my bones, but words will never hurt me," but for me, living with emotional pain is more painful than death.

While making changes, I often felt depressed and sad for all the time that I wasted sitting in prison as the result of my violence. However, in 2005, things happened that gave me a new view on my life and helped with my depression.

I mentioned that God had been responsible for the awakening that inspired my transformation. Although I kept praying, I did not get involved in organized religion until I was transferred to a medium-security prison in BC. It was there that I really started to get involved with volunteers and going to chapel services. After these baby steps and a transfer to a minimum-security institution, I began working as the chapel clerk. I became really involved in helping with the organization of chapel events and helping guys transition to minimum-security from medium-security. Even though they were physically inside a minimum, their mindset was not there, making the transition difficult. Walking around a yard that has no fences can be strange and quite the challenge. I have to admit that the men who adapted with the most enthusiasm were the lifers. The reason is very simple: men who have been incarcerated for more than a decade appreciate that small sense of freedom. I still fear doing something wrong even when I am not doing anything out of line; a result of being under a microscope for so many years.

In this minimum, a few other lifers and I formed an outreach committee. The goal of the committee was to bring more guys into the chapel. One Saturday, we were having a prayer group and I volunteered to introduce a Christian music video called, "You Are Not Alone." I stood up, not quite knowing what I was going to say. As I started speaking, I heard myself explaining that because I had been in prison for over 20 years, everyone that I had known before had moved on with their lives. I had no friends, acquaintances, or family outside the prison walls. Even my dear brother Luc felt the need to move on with his life; he had cut ties with me a few years before in 2008. I explained to the group that the only relationship that was not over for me was my relationship with God.

As I sat back in my chair, I was troubled. The realization that I had lost everyone in my life because of my actions was devastating. I don't blame them for leaving. I even cut off some relationships myself. Others just got tired of waiting. By committing murder, I had also committed social suicide.

A few days later, I was talking with a friend in Bible study, and he reminded me about a story where Jesus Christ was talking to Nicodemus. Jesus was explaining that a man needed to be reborn again, true to the Holy Spirit. This image made me think about what was going on in my life and my heart.

Many of us have said that if we had only known then what we know now, things would have turned out differently. I have said that many times in my life. The story of Jesus and Nicodemus made me realize I was faced with a unique opportunity. Everyone that I had known before I came to prison had moved on, and, yes, this is sad. However, I had an opportunity at a brand-new start. When I return to society, no one will know me. How I present myself is how others will see me and get to know me. Instead of being perceived as a violent and dangerous person, I could recreate myself.

In 2003, I started attending the Alternatives to Violence Project (AVP), which is a group based on the principles of restorative justice. AVP is non-profit organization made up of volunteers from outside and inside the prison, who focus on living non-violent lives. This project began in the early 1970s in a New York State prison by a group of prisoners that called themselves the "Think Tank." They realized that younger prisoners were coming into the institution, and the violence was becoming more and more severe. These prisoners wanted to create safe spaces to explore the impacts of violence and to help others learn to live non-violent lives. They partnered with a group of Quakers to develop a series of experiential workshops to create community and explore skills related to nonviolence, such as communication skills, conflict resolution, and the deconstruction of stereotypes.

This project has been one of the most influential aspects of my growth into a more peaceful and caring person. In order to participate in AVP, I had to step out of my comfort zone and engage in a group process. This was difficult as I had become solitary in my transformation, making changes personally and privately, for the most part. To get more comfortable in a group setting, I needed to have some sense of control. To obtain this, I would arrive to an AVP workshop 45 minutes before the group started. I would form our circle of 20–25 chairs and just wait. I would sit in the room—which, ironically, was where parole hearings were held—in a chair facing the exit. I would stare at that exit sign wondering what the hell I was doing there. So many times, I wanted to bolt out of that exit door. However, once the first person walked in the door, I felt out of politeness, it was too late for me to leave. After a year or so, the feelings of wanting to escape subsided and I started to bring other prisoners to the workshops. I became a leader—facilitator, trainer, and coordinator—with AVP.

AVP has changed my life in a significant way. I have spent over 100 days in those AVP circles, both inside and outside of correctional institutions. I was trained as an AVP facilitator and was mentored by other more experienced facilitators until I was awarded my certificate as a qualified AVP facilitator in 2009. In this role, I help train and mentor other facilitators who are both prisoners and community members. One of the most important community supports I have is through a group I became a part of when I was still locked up. Through this project, I was able to stay connected with people who understand who I am, where I came from, and the issues I face. AVP is a unique and appealing initiative in prison because it is coordinated and facilitated together by volunteers and prisoners. Staff do not attend nor supervise our gatherings, and it is not considered a correctional program. Prisoners are not coerced to attend to look good for the parole board. It is a truly voluntary project—all of us who attend are working on ourselves and trying to support one another to live non-violent lives.

Over the years, I have gained many skills from AVP. By nature, I am shy and very reserved. I don't like to be the centre of attention. In AVP, we are invited to take turns sharing in a circle. This spotlight was very difficult for me, but I kept trying to speak up and share my truth. When I became a facilitator, my shyness impacted me. However, through working with other facilitators, I learned to be more confident in my skills and abilities. Some AVP workshops have included victims of serious and violent crime as volunteer participants. Hearing their stories made me so much more aware of the impact that my acts of violence had on others. These experiences helped me to put a face to my own victims. As I have become more aware of the impact of violence, I have shared this knowledge and helped others I was incarcerated with come to terms with their own experiences with violence. Being in circle with victims and other caring community members has brought me a great sense of humility and a connection to something greater than myself.

AVP also helped me to develop problem solving skills and the ability to look for a non-violent solution when faced with conflict. For someone immersed in a violent world for so long, instrumental violence has been an effective survival tool. Walking away from conflict in a prison is seen as a sign of weakness and it can make you vulnerable to victimization. For years, I used extreme violence to keep myself safe. When I first started my sentence, I would have never imagined I would be facilitating a group called "Alternatives to Violence." At one time, I didn't think alternatives existed.

Other groups, such as the Better Life Ministry and FAVOUR (Friends and Volunteers Offering Understanding and Restoration), have been other places where I could share my struggles and get support. I have learned so much about myself and the outside world through the relationships I have developed with volunteers. It has been amazing to continue to receive support from them upon my release.

After a lot of hard work and determination, this is how I presented myself to the Parole Board of Canada when I came up for release. Although these changes have not been easy, I have been able to push past the many fears that I had. The following section is based on a document I wrote just prior to seeing the board and presenting my case for freedom.

# MY FEARS

I thought I would feel differently facing the possibility of release after being locked up for decades, but I was scared. I feared being on the street. What if I can't make it? What is my place in the free world? I feared being alone, of being abused by people I had grown to love and trust. I had the same fears as a grown man as I did when I first entered a juvenile centre at 11. So much had changed, but the fear remained.

My fear to be released was based on my past, but also from watching people I did time with get parole and return to prison. It seemed the pressures of life outside were too much for them to handle. They told me stories of being treated unfairly by their community parole officers. This made me fear leaving the comfort zone that I had created for myself over the years in prison.

Being in prison gave me the stability I lacked on the street. In prison, I didn't have to worry about much. I wrote the following while doing time; I find it so interesting to reflect on after being on parole for nearly 7 years. It reminds me of the daily stresses I live with that replaced different types of stress during my incarceration.

**I don't have to pay rent or worry about shelter.**

Being homeless as a child, the idea of having a roof over my head each night is comforting.

**I don't have to worry about getting a job.**

On the street, I was only good enough to do manual labour. Working on the ships was the only legitimate job I ever had. In prison, I am the chapel clerk. I feel useful and appreciated for the work I do. It is a job I love, and I do it well.

**I don't have to worry about transportation.**

In prison, everything is walking distance. I have never had a licence or driven a car legally.

**I don't have to worry about my next meal.**

On the street, food was not always available. As a child, I had gone days without eating. Meals would come from take-out, other people, or a garbage can. I will always have food on my plate in prison. I learned to cook very well inside since completing the culinary arts program.

**I don't have to worry about having people around who will help and support me.**

On the street, I had nobody. I felt betrayed by adults, even those professionals like social workers who were paid to help me. Early in life, I chose solitude. Being alone meant not having to care about or answer to anyone. When you have nothing, you have nothing to lose.

**In prison, I always have someone I can talk to.**

I have been in prison for so long, I have trusted friends who are fellow prisoners and many volunteers who support me unconditionally. I have seen many volunteers come and go but they all share the same non-judgmental attitude.

**I don't have to worry about clothing.**

Clothing wasn't something I thought about much inside or outside prison. Almost all of the clothes I had in prison were handed down by other prisoners who were either leaving or getting rid of things they didn't wear.

**I don't have to worry about a gym membership.**

In prison, I could often see the gym from my cell window. I could work out any time I wanted, multiple times a day. People knew me in the weight pit—it was part of my identity.

**I don't have to worry about utility bills such as phone, electricity, water.** I don't have to worry about health or dental care. I don't even have to worry about retirement. All these expenses are taken care of inside. I could die in here and it wouldn't cost me a thing to be buried.

**I don't have to worry about people abusing me or taking advantage of me.**

Prison means safety for me. I carry my history of extreme violence and this protects me from predators. Prison is normal to me as it is where I have been for most of my life.

This list of things I don't worry about in prison is a guide to all that scared me about freedom. Leading up to my parole hearing, I was more scared to be released than of being denied and spending at least another year inside.

# CHAPTER 7 - STEPPING IN

*There are no hopeless cases, only hopeless methods.*

*Author unknown*

There are many people who lost hope for Yves and never believed he would be released from prison. Social workers, family members, doctors, and individuals working in corrections all gave up on him at one time or another. However, Yves has been living non-violently in the community since 2013. He has learned to live with the trauma of his childhood and the layers of trauma from long-term incarceration. Yves is not alone. Most people serving life sentences are released from prison and live peacefully as our neighbours, friends, and co-workers. However, doing life on the outside can be more challenging than living in prison. Reintegration is painful and difficult. People who have served long sentences are entering a world that only vaguely resembles the "outs" they remember.

"Cascading" is the gradual process of moving from high security levels to lower security levels. In Canada, lifers especially would never be released from a maximum-security environment straight to the street. The rationale for cascading is that the majority of prisoners have high treatment needs upon their admission to prison, and the experience of incarceration exacerbates their marginalization and trauma. Gradually removing the imposed limits on their freedom promotes more successful re-entry into communities.

By the time a lifer applies for parole, they have spent many years in maximum- and medium-security environments and are likely spending their days in a minimum-security level institution, which means living communally, preparing their own meals, and possibly spending some time in the community on Escorted Temporary Absences. However, no matter what level of security a person is living in, prison life is radically different than the outside world. Not only does the "convict code" still exist, but there is also a lack of privacy and autonomy, and constant threat of violence or transfer to higher levels of security.

Prison life is slow and structured. Prisoners have very few choices or responsibilities aside from following the countless rules—both formal and informal. On the outside, life is fast-paced, complex, and nearly limitless choices exist. Think about the hundreds of decisions the average citizen makes from the time one wakes up in the morning. While people on the outside also have many obligations, people on parole have even more. Parole conditions restrict many aspects of prisoner's lives, including who they see, what and when they report to a parole officer, where they live and work, and what must be avoided, such as alcohol, computer access, and specific people and locations. Parolees have many limits on their freedom while living amongst people with none.

Many lifers experience problems adjusting to the world past the bars. They will often struggle with employment, family reunification, finding friends, subjugation to criminal labels, temptations around substances, and feeling isolated and alone—even in large cities. Many lifers will say it feels as if they have a sign over their heads notifying everyone that they came from prison. The stigma—both real and imagined—is incredibly stressful.

People think about parole as stepping out of prison. I think of it as stepping in, stepping into your world and out of mine. These two worlds could not be more different. Prison rules and our way of life do not fit out here. I was much more scared to be released into the community in my 50s than I was entering prison as a scrawny 20-year-old.

The process of conditional release or parole in Canada is a complicated one that most of the public knows nothing about. However, parole is something lifers like me spend a lot of time thinking about. My first-degree murder charge carried a mandatory minimum sentence of life 25, which meant I waited 23 years to make my first parole application. Others who are not doing life in prison but are serving a specific number of years can apply for some form of conditional release much earlier in their sentence.

Parole is an integral part of corrections in Canada and is also known as graduated release or cascading. As someone moves through the system, the intention is that they transition from higher levels of security to lower levels as their risk to re-offend is reduced through correctional interventions and time. Even prisoners who do not apply for early release will be supervised in the community on mandatory supervision. This gradual release can be contrasted with "cold turkey release," where someone goes directly from prison to the community.

Many people believe that prisoners should serve every day of their sentence inside and walk out the front door when their sentence is done. This so-called "truth in sentencing" argument has led to the abolition of parole in many American states. However, this get-tough approach leads to a false sense of security. People released directly to the community without support and supervision lack the resources they need to be able to adapt to the vast differences between prison life and society. This increases the risk of re-offending and makes everyone less safe.

Graduated release means that over time, lifers will have gone through various security levels and reached a minimum-security prison setting before taking the next step into the community. I spent 1 week short of 8 years in a minimum-security prison until I was released on day parole on December 6, 2013, after serving a little less than 32 years in total.

According to CSC, plans for release begin the moment someone's sentence begins. Despite this stated mission, the reality is different for lifers. It can be decades before we will be released, so lifers are given low priority for correctional programs. No matter what our risk level is assessed at, it is mandatory for all lifers to spend the first 2 years of their sentence in maximum-security where programs are limited anyway. For the first part of a life sentence, we are warehoused with no programming and very little to do. Punished by deprivation of liberty and again by boredom, those first years are agony.

Upon entering prison, all prisoners are assigned a case management team who assess risk levels and creates a correctional plan. According to CSC, the correctional plan is a document that outlines a risk management strategy for each offender. It specifies those interventions and monitoring techniques required to address areas associated with the risk to re-offend. The plan usually involves certain restrictions on movement and actions, as well as commitments to participate in activities such as jobs and correctional programs. Since each offender has different needs and problems, each plan is different.

The correctional plan helps determine the security level someone is placed in and how their time will be spent there. While this formal process is happening, each prisoner is creating their own correctional plan in their minds. When I look back, my plans changed throughout my sentence as I adapted to the reality of doing time. I had to adjust how I perceived other inmates as I went down security levels. In a maximum-security environment, I would never speak to a sexual offender or an informant. In a minimum, we had to find ways to co-exist. At first, the focus of my personal correctional plan was survival but as the years went on, my goal became bettering myself in the hopes of release.

When I got my first life sentence, the furthest thing from my mind was preparing to be in front of the Parole Board of Canada. This would be as ridiculous as asking a child in kindergarten to think about their plans for retirement. At the start of this sentence, it was all I could do to open my eyes in the morning knowing I was facing decades in prison.

The transformation I describe in this book helped me survive behind prison fences because I was able to find hope. These changes began in my own heart and mind, with some help from the divine. Once these changes began, I knew I needed to reach out as I created a new life on my own.

My biggest fears about getting out in the community were fitting in, getting a job, and building a social network. Although I knew it was necessary to start to connect with other people, it was difficult because the years of abuse taught me that nobody could be trusted. It was slow at first, but I found the more open I was with people, the more I felt accepted. It became easier to trust as I learned there were people in the world that would not abuse me.

I am thankful for the various supports that I cultivated over the years. I would not have been released from prison or coped as well as I have without the caring people who believed in me and wanted to see me succeed. Not only do I have support from volunteers that I met while in prison, but the staff at the halfway house where I was first released were very helpful. My Community Case Management Team—including my parole officer, psych-nurse, psychologist, and even some of the office staff—have been crucial to helping me when I stumble and have encouraged me never to give up.

Despite this support, coming back out into this world after spending so much time behind the walls has been a very difficult experience. I feel like I am constantly playing catch-up, but I know I am not alone. I have tried to change on my own before and have failed. I am so grateful to every person that believed enough in me to encourage me to keep trying. These wonderful people took the time to help me learn about this world that had previously been so scary and hostile to me.

## *First Steps*

My first step into the community was in the form of an Escorted Temporary Absence (ETA). These passes provide opportunities for prisoners to spend a specific amount of time (no more than 12 hours) in the community under supervision at an approved location. Prisoners are usually supervised by a correctional staff member or a community volunteer. These absences are granted for several reasons, including medical treatment, personal development, family contact, volunteer work, vocational training, or for spiritual purposes. The main purpose for these short periods of time out of prison is to begin the painful process of community reintegration.

My first ETA was to Simon Fraser University to attend a presentation honouring Dr. Liz Elliott, who passed away from cancer in 2011. Liz was a criminology professor at SFU who was dedicated to restorative and prison justice. She was a brilliant advocate with a keen sense of justice for prisoners. I met Liz through participating in AVP, and she remained a dear friend for many years. A couple of days before she died, she came to the prison to see me. It was a difficult and emotional visit as I could see she was in pain. Her lively face was now gaunt and greyish, and she had lost so much weight. As sick as she was, she still took the time to enter prison to see another lifer and me. It meant so much to me that she came, and the last thing I told her was that I would continue this life of non-violence and promised to talk to universities and share my story. Students meant just as much to her as prisoners, and I wanted to let her know I would continue to serve them when she was gone.

It was an honour to be able to attend the ceremony for Liz, but I remember feeling anxious waiting for the van to arrive at the prison administration building to pick me up. I was leaving my comfort zone, and the unknown that awaited me was nerve-wracking. Luckily, the correctional staff member who accompanied me on this pass was someone I knew well. She was on my case management team. She understood that this first pass would be difficult and reassured me that each time would get easier.

The drive from Mission to Burnaby Mountain that lasted well over an hour gave me a lot of time to think. As we entered the halls of the university, the number of people rushing around was overwhelming. As my eyes and heartrate adjusted, I began noticing some peculiar things. A student walking by tossing his bright turquoise hair over his shoulder. Hundreds of young people rushing through the halls, narrowly avoiding collisions with one another, their eyes glued to the cell phone in their hand. The number of "regular people" with visible tattoos was odd but not as weird as the student who walked by with a fake tail sticking out of his pants. I wondered what world I had stepped into.

When I was a child, I would often wonder what it would be like to fall asleep and wake up in the future. At that time, in my mind, the future was the year 2000. Sometimes I dreamt of this future out of curiosity, and other times to escape bad moments. Strangely, being released from prison allowed me to live this experience of time travel. The only difference between travelling in a time machine and doing a life sentence is that you can see the world change from prison, although you are not a part of it. I saw society transform through my television set, newspapers, and magazines. Sometimes people who visited would provide clues about what was happening in the free world, but I hadn't been participating in the rapid changes in technology, society, politics, and the economy for decades.

My time at the university that day was a blur, and before I knew it, I was back at the prison getting ready for lights out. Although this first ETA was stressful, it was more enjoyable as I was surrounded by caring people—many of whom I knew as volunteers in the institution. The correctional officer had been right; the ETAs that followed got much easier. I began attending church and completed a 60-day work release as a cook at the Chilliwack Community Correctional Centre, a CSC-run halfway house. All of these experiences helped prepare me for my release. I spent many months drafting out a release plan with my parole officer. This package of information would be considered by the parole board prior to my hearing. I was taking the next step to freedom, and it felt very good.

## *The Gatekeepers: Facing the Parole Board of Canada*

Despite the gruesome things I have faced in my life, I feared the parole process a great deal. Your fate is in the hands of strangers, and during the hearing, you are expected to calmly discuss the traumatic things that you have done to others. I knew the board would be interested not only in my release plan but also in my extensive criminal history and over 30 years of incarceration. There was a lot of ground to cover, and I knew I had to be in touch with everything about myself, so I could clearly communicate the journey I had been on to become the non-violent man that was sitting in front of them.

Both parole and court hearings are stressful, but there is a major difference. In court, you only have the right to speak to state your plea and make a statement before sentencing; your lawyer handles all other court procedure. In a parole hearing, you can have an assistant or a lawyer to support you, but you are expected to speak on your own behalf. Although I had gotten much more comfortable speaking in public, it was still a challenge for me to articulate myself in front of strangers.

Similar to court, you are walking into in a room of people whose decision will impact your life in profound ways. Many people think that our destiny is in our hands, but it is not that simple when you are serving life. I am the property of the federal government and, as such, they could keep me in prison forever. I had to prove through documentation and my verbal presentation that I am no longer a threat to the community. If the board perceived any threat to public safety, I would not be released.

The more violent your crime, the more you need to demonstrate that you are fully aware of your triggers and understand exactly what brought you to commit such harmful acts. You must be able to address questions like:

1. What is your understanding of your crime?
2. How can you make sure that this will never happen again?
3. How can we be assured that the public is safe with you living in the community?
4. What kind of support/resources do you have in the community to help you reintegrate after having spending so many years in institutions?
5. Do you have a backup plan if things start to go wrong and you find yourself in the same situation? If so, what is the plan?

I attended the parole hearing with a lawyer who understood a lot about long-term incarceration. She was also a supporter who had known me for years, so it made me a little more comfortable to have her at my side. The parole officer I had been working with was a French-speaking woman who put me at ease by conversing with me in my mother tongue. She helped prepare a comprehensive release plan and fully supported my application for parole.

Walking in with two supports by my side, I sat across the table from the three board members and stenographer who were already seated. It was a sunny day, but I didn't let the beautiful weather get my hopes up. Even though I had worked hard to get to this point, there was no guarantee of my release. I am not an arrogant man, and don't assume anyone owes me any favours for the destruction I have caused over the years.

The parole board members were professional and asked many important questions that I was able to answer. I didn't feel judged or attacked as others I have heard do in this process. It felt like the goal of the hearing was to learn more about the changes I had made. They asked me for details about my release plan, and I explained how hard I had worked to solidify community support, a halfway house that would accept me through my proven track record as a professional cook, and the psychological care I would continue to receive. I described what I would do if I felt things were going sideways. I articulated my willingness to reach out and accept help and how I was accountable for the harm I had caused over the years.

After over an hour of discussion, the board adjourned to review the information and come up with a decision. I waited in the visiting room, feeling anxious about the result but confident in how I presented myself. I knew that I would never need to remember what I had said because I told the truth. I was accountable, direct, and listened carefully to their questions and concerns. I was willing to accept any decision that the board arrived at. I knew if I were not granted release this time, the board would provide suggestions of areas I could work on to increase the chances of being successful for my next parole board appearance in one year.

When I heard that I was granted day parole, I was happy beyond imagination. It is impossible to explain the joy I felt at the prospect of freedom after over three decades in captivity. I also felt numb as my body and mind felt overwhelmed with disbelief that this day had finally come. It might be the same feeling a dog has after running after cars all day and finally catching one: he has no idea what to do with it.

I felt deeply grateful to everyone who helped me through this process: my parole assistant that guided me through such a stressful and complicated process, and my case management team, friends, and volunteers that encouraged me to face my demons and take this next step. Sitting there, absorbing the parole board's decision to release me, I remembered all the times that I wondered whether I should even try to get out. I often questioned if I would ever be able to cope outside of these institutions where I felt safe. As much as I felt elated, there was also underlying worry that I might fail and disappoint everyone who supported and believed in me. I put these feelings aside and allowed myself to be happy in this moment in the sunshine.

# *The Sweet & Sour Taste of Freedom*

Like most things with corrections, the process of release involves a lot of paperwork. Usually, it is just a hassle, but this paperwork was different. So different, in fact, the process of filling it out is called a "parade."

I was called into the Admission & Discharge Department of the prison where I was given a paper with the names of various departments around the institution. I took this paper on "parade," visiting all the departments listed and obtaining signatures to confirm my "business" with them was complete. These papers confirmed I had no overdue library books, institutional property such as bedding was returned, my canteen account was closed, and that finance had cut a cheque for any money I had accumulated in my prison account. These parades are something every prisoner dreams about. As I completed mine, it felt more real that I was leaving prison behind.

After the parade, I headed to my cell to pack it up. I was surprised to see just how much stuff I had accumulated over the 8 years I had been inside that institution. Some things I took with me, some I gave to friends.

Within a few days, a correctional officer drove me to the halfway house. It was a relief to be in a familiar environment where I recognized faces from my work release. Chilliwack Community Correctional Centre (CCCC) is a little different from other halfway houses as it is run by CSC rather than a non-profit organization. Although the building is surrounded by trees and a beautiful lawn, inside there is a bit of an institutional feel, which I found comforting. Not exactly a prison, but it had familiar protocols and furniture. The staff did not wear uniforms and you could leave by simply signing your name on a piece of paper and walking out the door. This was something I would need to get used to. When I first arrived, I had a meeting with some of the staff, and they reviewed the behavioural expectations, rules, services, and available supports. I had to stay inside for the week as part of the adjustment process. I was OK with that as I didn't really want to go outside anyway.

It was a couple of weeks before I felt brave enough to go venture to the corner store. I felt lost in this new community as I had never lived in BC outside of an institution. Although I had been on the outside many times on ETAs, there was always a volunteer or staff member with me. Now I was completely alone. The city noise, traffic, and strange faces were overwhelming, and I quickly retreated back to the Centre.

I spent 2 and a half years at CCCC. Eventually, I was given full parole from the Parole Board of Canada, which meant I could move in with my then-girlfriend Kim. I still had many parole restrictions, but I didn't mind. I was taking another step into this free world, and this time, I had a wonderful woman beside me.

## Peaks & Valleys

Being released from prison after all those years was like walking into a Star Trek episode. The advances in technology have been my favourite part of my new life. I love computers, tablets, cellphones/smartphones, smart watches, Bluetooth, GPS, and all the electronic gadgets in cars today. I truly appreciate all these tools and how much I can learn about the world by accessing them.

I enjoy some things that other people out here despise, like sitting in traffic. From prison, I would watch the news on TV and see cars lined up for miles. All I wanted to do was be one of those drivers. My commute to and from work, which can be at least an hour both ways, is a time of peace that brings a feeling of well-being. I am grateful to have a job to go to and a car to sit in gridlock in.

While there are countless things I enjoy about being free, I don't think anything could have prepared me for the cost of living in 2013. The price of rent, food, gas, and water shocked me. Water out of the tap is clean and free, and watching people buy bottled water makes me think we are living in a post-nuclear world.

I paid $4.50 for my first ham and cheese sandwich on the outside. No sides, no pickle, no juice, no salad. When I tried to order my first coffee and needed a menu to do so, my mind was blown. When I was out of prison last, the choices were decaf or regular, cream and sugar. Now there are a hundred choices of coffee. Eventually, I found a solution by ordering a French Vanilla from Tim Horton's. I don't have to add any sugar or milk, which makes it very simple.

The vast number of choices that I am faced with every day remain difficult. Inside prison, choices are very limited and often made for you. You are told when to get up, when to work, what to eat, where to be and for how long, and what to wear. Out here, there are so many more choices to make, and I often find decision making exhausting.

After spending three decades in prison, I knew finding employment would be a challenge. I do very well in interviews as I present professionally and am well-spoken. I am qualified for the work I apply for. However, at the end of most interviews, when asked if they will find anything on a criminal record check, I tell them I have spent almost 32 years inside prisons across Canada. After hearing this, the interview changes direction. I watch the interviewer's attitude change as they looked both scared and worried. I understand the feelings that someone would have with me sitting in their office after making such a statement. I appreciate that any potential employer would have questions and concerns about their staff and customers should they hire someone with my history.

Through some existing connections, I have been able to try several jobs since being released. My first job was in a fast-food restaurant. This brings a smile to my face because in prison often you will hear guys close to release say, "If I have to flip burgers to make it out there I will." I said it and I did just that, flip burgers.

I also worked in construction, meat packaging, and traffic control. I now work full time in a production plant where I receive good benefits and holiday time. I am a respected employee and hard worker. I take none of these experiences for granted and seek to learn something new each day.

Gaining successful employment has been due to the help of friends and volunteers who form a support team around me. These relationships began in prison and have continued now that I am free. They are key to getting out and staying out.

## *Staying Out*

Besides technology, work, faith, and friendships, the most powerful influence in my life since leaving prison has been my wife, Kim. The possibility of meeting a woman like Kim is what helped me stay motivated to be released from jail. I had learned to live without freedom, sex, certain foods, and deep friendship, but I could not live without the love of a woman.

When I got out, I was not interested in a one-night stand. I wanted more. So, in this new world of technology, I did what others were doing and turned to the internet to meet someone. I built a profile on Plenty of Fish and soon connected with the most wonderful, beautiful, kind, loving woman that I have ever met. I fell in love with Kim very quickly. She is an intelligent, compassionate woman, and a loving mother.

Kim and I are the same age, but we have lived very different lives. Before meeting me, she had never crossed paths with anyone involved in the criminal world. Until very recently, Kim's philosophy on criminals was the same as many people: "Lock them all up and throw away the key!"

Given my past, Kim asked a lot of questions and expressed concerns as she had a family of her own, including three daughters, one son, and three grandchildren. Kim wasn't going to let a man with my history come into her home right away; she had a family to protect and care for. Kim wanted to know everything about my past, but, most importantly, she wanted to know about the man who was sitting in front of her today. I answered every question that Kim asked, and I was completely truthful. To keep seeing each other, Kim had to meet my Community Parole Officer. My parole officer was very supportive of our relationship, and Kim's family has accepted me into their lives.

I continue to be an active member of my faith group and volunteer often with AVP. I had a recent experience of being let back inside prison to facilitate a workshop with incarcerated men. It was my dream to be able to take what I have learned through AVP and help others. I feel so grateful for the opportunity to do so and will continue to go back inside as a helper as long as they will let me.

## Walk with Me

A question that I am often asked is, "How can we help people that have been incarcerated reintegrate back in the community?" There is not one easy answer, but, in my experience, what worked was having people in my life who knew some of my traumatic history and what I needed upon release. Having people stay in my life from prison into the community was one of the main reasons I was able to succeed out here.

Like many incarcerated people, I didn't have a healthy life prior to coming to prison. I had no strong emotional ties, no fixed address, little vocational training, no money management, or basic life skills. In prison, I addressed many of these shortcomings by achieving a high school diploma, taking college courses through correspondence, and building some cognitive and vocational skills through prison programming. Having said that, no prison programs prepared me for the world I walked into. It was the people who supported me and stood by me through my achievements and my stumbles.

Not everyone makes it in the community as a lifer. Although we reoffend at very low rates, our rates of suicide and health related issues are higher than the general population. A very good friend of mine took his own life within months of being released from prison. He was a lifer like me and my roommate at the halfway house. He was kind, intelligent, and had a good education, a skilled trade, and a well--paying job in his field. He had a supportive and loving family and had recently bought a house. When I heard he had died by suicide, I was stunned. I couldn't understand why he would have done this. It just shows that some of the trauma we live with cannot be seen on the outside. These scars are deep and invisible. I wish I could have done something to prevent this from happening.

I have had my own experiences with suicide. Although I have a wonderful support group and a wife who loves me unconditionally, in January of 2017, I tried to take my life by overdosing on antidepressants. Pills in hand, I couldn't stop thinking about all the harm I had caused others. The depression became too much, and I wanted to shut down. I am not proud of my actions that night. Still, I am grateful Kim and others stuck with me through this darkness, including my parole officer who sent me for counselling and a medication adjustment, rather than back to prison. If I had been found guilty of a parole breach, I would have spent a year in prison before I could re-apply to the parole board, and there would have been no guarantee that I would have been rereleased. I would have lost everything I had worked for. As a lifer with my history, if I go back in, they never had to let me out. I live under the dark cloud of this reality every day.

Strangely, I feel that something positive came out of that low point in my new life of freedom. By surviving that overdose, I realized that I had not lived up to my mantra of "no more victims." Had I taken my life, I would have caused immense pain for many people who believed in me: volunteers, friends, correctional staff, and the parole board who gave me the chance to make a new life. I would have broken the hearts of Kim and her loving family who let me into their lives, our innocent grandchildren who I adore with all my heart. The family that we have created cannot be added to my list of victims.

I am not perfect and still experience deep depression. I came to prison full of trauma and lived for over 30 years in an environment where violence was omnipresent. I spent most of my life being treated as a number, deprived of basic human dignity, and isolated. These conditions exacerbated the post-traumatic stress disorder (PTSD) I developed as a child. PTSD does not go away, and life outside institutions is often difficult. At Easter in 2020, I stumbled again. I wrote this letter to my supports explaining what happened.

*Dear friends,*

*I am writing this letter because I have been struggling very much in the last few months. My stressors have been building up and I have been having difficulties dealing with all of this.*

*I was locked up at the Chilliwack RCMP detachment for 48 hours on Easter Sunday. I was released on the following Tuesday. I was detained because of a breach of my parole conditions.*

*On Easter Saturday, feeling really depressed and overwhelmed with a lot of the stressors in my life, I went to visit a friend and started to feel really depressed. I started to drink one beer after another. After a couple, I thought that I might as well keep drinking because I realized that I had already fucked up—one or twelve doesn't make a difference on fucking up. I didn't want to risk driving my vehicle anywhere, especially under the influence. I haven't drunk for so many years, and not having had anything to eat all day, the drinking really hit me hard. I ended up sleeping there on their couch.*

*There was also very poor cell reception, and I didn't communicate at all with my wife, Kim. Kim was extremely concerned about my whereabouts; she didn't know if I had committed suicide, ran off the road, and was lying at the bottom of a ditch or ravine somewhere. What I have done is extremely selfish and irresponsible. My bad choice of actions that Easter Saturday in dealing with my stressors and depression was out of character for me. I am truly sorry for having put Kim, her family, and all of my support group through hell by not having been able to deal with this in a better way.*

*It is simple to say that this proves that I am only human, but no, I should have known better. This incident has made me realize that one of the contributing factors for this shortcoming is that I have been trying to deal with some issues by myself. In the last few years, I have been distancing myself from the support group that I have built over the years.*

*I have now realized that I need to reconnect and tighten my support group. Realizing that I can't do this on my own, I can't deal with all my stressors all at once. I can deal with those stressors when they are one at a time, but when I let them pile up, I get extremely overwhelmed, and my depression goes into overdrive. Unfortunately, I have a difficult time opening up and sharing my weaknesses because I don't want to burden anyone. That's the reason that my response to, "How are you, Yves?" is usually "fine."*

*So, I am reaching out to all of you in the hope that I haven't lost your friendship, trust, love, and support. I am truly sorry if I have let any one of you down. I'm so grateful to have my dear wife Kim by my side to support me through these difficult times, but my wife cannot be my only support—because of my history, this is way too much for even her to handle. That is the reason why I need to reconnect with all of you.*

*Thank you.*
*Sincerely yours, Yves*

This was a low point, and there will be others, but I did what I promised the parole board I would do, and I reached out. It is difficult to admit that you are struggling with basic things that others wouldn't even think about. It is also hard to live with vulnerability and the fear of failing everyone who believes in you. I know that I will struggle with these issues for the rest of my life.

There are things more important than freedom that will help me cope with my trauma and leave institutional life behind. The relationships I have built with my wife and her family, as well as all of those who support me will hold me up. Prison is no longer an option, and there will be no more victims.

# AFTERWORD - WORDS FROM FRIENDS & SUPPORTERS

I met Yves in 2014, a couple of months after he was out on day parole. I was intrigued by his story, yet cautious. I offered to help him navigate life on the outside. At that time, I had never known anyone who spent any length of time in prison. The first thing I noticed was his soft-spoken nature, his openness regarding his life choices and experiences, as well as his incredible self-awareness. I could see that he had done many years of self-reflection and work on himself to understand what brought him to spend 32 years in prison. I could also see that he was filled with anxiety about this new world, which was foreign to him. He was eager to find work and start a new life for himself. He is a man who actually meant what he said when he stated he was willing to work any job, even if it meant flipping burgers. (Which was his first job after he was released.) He just wanted to be a regular citizen who worked hard and payed taxes, like everyone else. He was goal oriented and had a drive to succeed like no one else I had met.

We married in 2016. His growth over the past years has been extraordinary. It hasn't been easy; no, there have been many hurdles we've had to overcome. However, we've learned along the way and continue to grow stronger.

Yves is an incredible man. He is my rock, my hero. He's a beautiful person today. I believe he is now the man he was meant to be, had tragedy not hit his family when he was just a 5-year-old boy. He has taught me so much and enriched my life. I have met many beautiful-soul people through Yves' circle of dear friends.

Because of Yves, I have learned to be grateful for everything in my life. He has shown me life through the eyes of a man locked up for most of his life. He takes nothing for granted. He's grateful for a roof over his head; freedom to go out for a coffee is bliss to Yves. Being stuck in rush hour traffic is a gift to Yves, as it means he has a job and he has a vehicle. Most of all, we are both grateful to have each other. Yves has taught me patience and resilience. He is a survivor. He has turned a hell of a violent life in the past completely around to becoming a caring, insightful, giving member of the community. He works hard every day and volunteers to speak to university students on his own time in the hopes of encouraging positive change in the penal system. He also spends many hours of his free time facilitating Alternative to Violence Project (AVP) workshops and training facilitators.

The man I know today is warm-hearted, sensitive, caring, humble, generous, and wise. He is courageous to share his story in the hopes of helping others. He has grown and matured over the past years. Anyone who knows Yves loves him. My family has adopted him and love him too. He enjoys his grandchildren as he sees what life should have been like when he was a child. They love their grandpa Yves. We all love his great sense of humour too!

Yves is my inspiration. Knowing Yves has led me to become a better person myself. I am grateful to have such a loving, supportive husband. I am proud of him for his many years of writing finally becoming a book. You got this, Yves!

- Kim Banner (Yves wife)

Imagine Arnold Schwarzenegger as the "Terminator" having a bad day in prison. Imagine the Prison Chaplain clerk working faithfully each day. Imagine a "Lifer" offering "life insights" to wide-eyed university students and intently interested university professors. Imagine 30,000 words describing this journey.

As a CSC Chaplain who "did time" ministering to many guys over 15 years, it is my profound pleasure to say congratulations Yves Cote and thank you for allowing me to walk alongside you from time to time. The "journey" I described above took courage, took will power, but ultimately took God's love. Death and rebirth occurred. All the best, Yves, as you continue to positively change our world!

- Reverend Leon Remus

Yves was on my caseload from 2005 to 2013. During that time, Yves was not a troublesome inmate. On the contrary, he was quiet, respectful, participated in programs, and was a wise individual. He was trusted by fellow inmates and staff alike. I will never forget, one day, Yves was watching the news' traffic report. He said to me, "I want to be stuck in traffic." It was his way of saying that he wanted to be part of society. Well, now, Yves is privileged to be stuck in traffic and I wish him well.

- Rachel Bunt, retired correctional officer.

We first met Yves at a medium-security prison as prison volunteers. Yves presented as a tough scary guy with an impressive display of muscles and tattoos and a disruptive sense of humour that helped him hide his insecurity and vulnerability. Yves caught himself playing games, apologized for his disrespectful behaviour, pledged to take things seriously and learn what he could. Yves came to understand how his childhood traumas led to his criminal thinking and behaviour and metamorphosed himself into an open and honest person with the ability to maintain healthy meaningful relationships and contribute to society. It's now been almost 20 years and we are happy to call Yves a friend for life.

- Larry Moore & Cathie Douglas, Heartspeak Productions

I met Yves through a chaplaincy outreach in the Fraser Valley several years ago. He was polite, kind, and reserved. Right away, I sensed a hope and a desire in him to live and contribute positively in our city despite the many obstacles he still would face. In just a few short years, I have watched Yves develop many friendships, support a family, and learn hard lessons about trust and starting over in an ever-changing world. Despite these challenges, he has been able to share his sense of humour with so many people. Our coffee time together was encouraging to both of us and I have been richly blessed having Yves in my life.

- Kevin Merz, Better Life Ministries

In my role as a Chaplain, I have known and worked with Yves for over 15 years, when he was still in the institution and during his release into the community. Yves has always impressed me as a man who has done a lot of work on himself in coming to grip with his crimes and then wanting to move on from them to make a positive contribution to society. I have walked with him through his ups and downs and adjustments back into society. I had the privilege of performing his wedding ceremony to his wonderful partner Kim. One of the foremost desires that Yves has expressed to me over the years has been to use his life and experience to influence others, and especially youth to learn from his mistakes and not follow in his path. To that end, a couple of years ago, I invited Yves to speak to the youth group at our church. Recently, I was in a conversation with one of the youth that attended Yves' talk and she said it the most interesting and informative talk she has every participated in and that all of the youth were captivated and paid keen attention to what Yves had to say to them. So I highly recommend Yves' book to you and through this book may Yves' desire and dream to inform and influence others for good continue to become a reality.

- Reverend Don Isben, Retired CSC Chaplain

When Yves and I first crossed paths, we observed each other from across the crowd. We had both spent our adult lives in the prison setting, an environment fraught with trials and tribulations, but it was not this commonality alone that caused us to acknowledge one another. Rather, it was a shared experience and journey in pursuit of a correct relationship with oneself, others, and the world around us that brought us together. I have come to admire Yves for his courage, truth-telling, and his commitment toward a transformed life. I look upon Yves as a friend and a person who is a positive influence in my life.

- Jim Reilly, British Columbia Corrections Branch, Adult Custody Division (1982-2019)

Yves came into my life over 15 years ago when I was volunteering as a sponsor visiting prisoners under the organization M2-W2, a prison visitation ministry.

When I first met Yves, he was a pretty scary looking individual, but God instantly gave me a love for him. Over the years, as my husband and I visited him in prison, we saw a gradual change in his appearance and a growth in his faith. It has been a blessing for us to witness what the Lord has done in his life. My prayers for him are for him to see God using his book and his life to inspire others to become friends with lonely men and women in prison and encourage them as they serve their time.

- Alice Chambers, M2-W2, a prison visitation ministry

# REFERENCES

Baranyi, G., Cassidy, M., Fazel, S, Priebe, S, & Mundt, A. (2018). Prevalence of Posttraumatic Stress Disorder in Prisoners, *Epidemiologic Reviews,* 40(1), pp. 134–145.

Elliott, E. (2011). *Security with care: Restorative justice and healthy societies.* Halifax, NS: Fernwood Publishing.

Kouyoumdjian, F., Schuler, A., Matheson, F. I., & Hwang, S. W. (2016). Health status of prisoners in Canada: Narrative review. *Canadian family physician*, 62(3), pp. 215–222.

Llewellyn J. & Downie, J. (2011). Introduction. In J. Llewellyn & J. Downie (Eds.), *Being relational: Reflections on relational theory and health, law and policy* (pp. 1-12). Vancouver, BC: UBC Press.

Pranis, K., Stuart, B., & Wedge, M. (2003). *Peacemaking circles: From crime to community.* St. Paul, MN: Living Justice Press.

White, R. & Graham, H. (2010). *Working with Offenders: A guide to concepts & practices.* New York, NY: Willan Publishing.

# ABOUT THE AUTHORS

## *Yves Côté*

My name is Yves Réal Côté. Since the age of 11, I have spent most of my life in institutions. I am what is known as a "lifer" serving the most severe sentence available in Canada; life in prison without the possibility of parole for 25 years. That means I will be under supervision by the government of Canada until my death. I am actually serving *two* of these life sentences. My crimes consist of the use of violence in the community and in prison. In 1989, I took a life in Ottawa and was convicted of first-degree murder. In 1995, I received another life sentence for a murder I committed in 1993 while imprisoned in a maximum-security institution. Two days after having been found guilty of the first murder and sentenced to life in prison, I received another sentence of 14 years for two bank robberies and one year for attempting to escape prison. After serving nearly 32 years in prison, on December 6, 2013, I was released on day parole to reside in a halfway house. In 2016, I received full parole and today I live with my wife and work full-time in the Fraser Valley of beautiful British Columbia. I am a loving man and a responsible, contributing citizen.

Writing this book is part of the transformative process I have been going through for many years.

I have done time in 18 different federal institutions across Canada at every level of security; minimum-security, medium-security, maximum-security, and super-maximum known as the Special Handling Unit (SHU). I am covered with tattoos and some say that I portray a threatening image, an evil look. In the "outside" world, I will likely never pass as "normal." This façade is the direct result of adapting to the prison world. However, the majority of people who take the time to have a conversation with me see me as a very intelligent man who has made a positive impact in the world and continues to help others. It would be such a waste if my painful life experiences were not shared with the intention of reducing the current and future suffering of others.

I strongly believe that sharing my story can make a difference. I have spoken in numerous university and community settings and received heart-felt feedback. I would have never thought that it would be possible for me to make such a positive impact on others. Some people told me that hearing my story reduced their prejudice towards offenders and prison. Others said they were scared to death when they learned that a murderer would be addressing them. After hearing what I had to say, their fear had completely disappeared.

I have handwritten hundreds of pages over the years I spent in prison, many of them during my time in solitary confinement. I have kept writing since my release. This book contains a snapshot of my life and my thoughts on many topics. Some of what I have written may shock certain people and, if you feel offended, I apologize in advance. My purpose is not to please or to displease anybody nor trash anyone or the criminal justice system. Although some of my reflections may seem negative, my goals are to share my truth, take responsibility for my actions, and, perhaps, help and inspire others in their change.

I am a simple man writing about making changes, friendship, love, religion, crime and punishment, and, naturally, incarceration. Many parts of this book have been very difficult and even re-traumatizing to write. However, in a society where it seems we have lost common sense to fear and everything seems artificial, I am convinced that this book will be able to help readers better understand the world in which prisoners live and what needs to change.

I have participated in countless programs while incarcerated. I achieved the equivalent of a high school diploma and have completed eight college courses in psychology, philosophy, and sociology. Despite years of correctional programs and some education, I am not an expert in any of the subjects that I am going to write about. However, I have enough lived experiences to give an informed opinion on topics that touch us all. I have asked my friend and colleague, Alana Abramson, to contribute some academic insights and help edit this work.

## Alana Abramson

My name is Alana Marie Abramson; I was born on the unceded, traditional territory of the Coast Salish peoples (Vancouver, British Columbia). I am of British, European, Metis, and Cree decent. My parents, Ian and Elaine, were born and raised in Vancouver. I am one of four children and I grew up in Surrey, British Columbia. Today, I am a guest living on unceded, traditional Secwepemc territory (Kamloops) and am a full-time criminology instructor at Kwantlen Polytechnic University. I am also a passionate advocate, researcher, and practitioner of restorative and transformative justice.

Despite the privilege of being born into a middle-class, two parent family, the road I have walked was not always easy. I found high school unchallenging and uninspiring at best and violent and victimizing at worst. I struggled with dramatic and unpredictable hormonal changes and victimization that led to rebellious and disrespectful behaviour. After being asked to leave both home and school, I lived on the streets of Vancouver where I experienced traumatic victimization, isolation, and substance misuse. I was arrested just before my 16th birthday and placed in foster care where I struggled to get my life on track. Through the support of caring people, I was able to reconcile with my parents and return home. I didn't know it then, but this was my first experience of restorative justice.

I was the first in my family to attend a post-secondary institution. I found a passion for criminology in my second year. In 2000, I met my mentor, Dr. Liz Elliott, after enrolling in a Restorative Justice course at Simon Fraser University. She introduced me to the Alternatives to Violence Project (AVP) at Mission Institution, medium-security. I became an active volunteer working alongside her, other community members, and federally sentenced people. AVP workshops provide a safe and inclusive opportunity for us to look at the violence in our past and work towards living non-violent lives. The labels of "offender" and "volunteer" are left at the door. Everyone in the circle is equal and treated with dignity as a human being. These experiences solidified my passion for transformative justice and penal abolition. Since then, I have dedicated myself to the values and practices of peacemaking and restorative justice.

Yves and I met in 2004 through Liz and AVP and have been friends and colleagues ever since. I was honoured when Yves asked if I would help him tell his story. My contributions consist of editing his original work, interviewing Yves to fill in the missing pieces, and providing some academic context. Stories are powerful vehicles for individual and social change and Yves has an important story to tell. This book is for social science students, researchers, and faculty, and anyone interested in trauma, transformation, and criminal justice.

CPSIA information can be obtained
at www.ICGtesting.com
Printed in the USA
BVHW022142020421
604061BV00022B/199/J